The View from Hawk Mountain

The View from Hawk Mountain

The Story of the World's First Raptor Sanctuary

MICHAEL HARWOOD

Illustrations by Fred Wetzel

STACKPOLE BOOKS

Published by
STACKPOLE BOOKS
5067 Ritter Road
Mechanicsburg, PA 17055
www.stackpolebooks.com

This book was originally published in 1973 by Charles Scribner's Sons.

Printed in the United States of America

Cover design by Wendy Reynolds
Cover photograph of Hawk Mountain Sanctuary © John McGrail / johnmcgrail.com
Cover photograph of golden eagle © Russ Kerr / majestyofbirds.com

10 9 8 7 6 5 4 3 2 1

First edition

Library of Congress Cataloging-in-Publication Data

Harwood, Michael.
    The view from Hawk Mountain / Michael Harwood.
        p. cm.
    Originally published: New York: Scribner, 1973.
    Includes bibliographical references.
    ISBN 0-8117-2976-1
    1. Birds of prey—Pennsylvania—Hawk Mountain Sanctuary. 2. Bird watching—Pennsylvania—Hawk Mountain Sanctuary. 3. Birds—Pennsylvania—Hawk Mountain Sanctuary. I. Title.

QL696.F3 H37 2001
598.9'09748'16—dc21   00-054926

To all the partakers of the view

Acknowledgments

I owe many thanks to all my friends at Hawk Mountain, particularly to the curator, Alexander C. Nagy, and to his wife, Arlene. Without their generosity and interest, *The View from Hawk Mountain* could not have been written. The same must be said about Maurice Broun, the pioneering curator emeritus, and his "keeper of the gate," Irma Broun; Maurice's early history of the sanctuary, *Hawks Aloft*, deserves a bow all its own.

Richard Sharadin and James Brett, assistant curators; Fred Wetzel, formerly assistant curator (his drawings grace this book); Barbara Lake, the sanctuary secretary—each have enlarged my experiences at Hawk Mountain. And so have innumerable other friends who have stared out into the eastern sky with me, watching the parade of passing hawks, especially David A. Titus, Herbert D. Hale, Ogden Goelet, Roger Pasquier, Louis Witkin, Carl D. Brandt, Gordon Lander, Franklin Haas, Robert C. Hughes, Thomas Mutchler, and the late Harold F. Burns. Mr. and Mrs. William Haas of Minersville were cheery hosts to a wandering birder.

The research for the book depended on many people: along with most of the above, Charles Mohl of Drehersville, Pennsylvania, Charles Thomas of Hamburg, and Sam Turner of Lenhartsville, who talked about Hawk Mountain as it was in the old days; George M. Sutton and Richard H. Pough, who offered recollections about the conservation movement's discovery of the gunning stands at the mountain; and Tom Hanson, one of the early Hawk Mountain volunteers. John J. Craighead, John R. Haugh, Gerald S. Mersereau, Donald A. Hopkins, Neil Currie, and Sidney A. Hessel supplied material and commentary on hawks and hawk migrations. Information and advice, particularly about the effects of pesticides on birds of prey, came from Joseph J. Hickey, Charles F. Wurster, Lucille F. Stickel, Sergej Postupalsky, Frances Hamerstrom, Mitchell A. Byrd, Stanley Wiemeyer, Jan Reese, Robert Senior Kennedy, Iola Gruchy, William Drury, and Ian C. T. Nesbit.

I am also greatly indebted to friends at National Audubon—Roland C. Clement, vice president for biology; Richard L. Plunkett, his assistant; Nancy T. Manson, librarian; and Sylvia S. Donohue, in the educational services department; to Marguerite B. Hoadley, Carol J. Simms, and Mary M. Fanning of the Gunn Memorial Library in Washington, Connecticut, who kept a constant stream of reference books coming my way in interlibrary loans from, it must have seemed, all over the Northeast; to Eleanor Stickney of the Peabody Museum of Natural History at Yale; to the staffs of the American Museum of Natural History library in New York and the Reading, Pennsylvania, Public Library; to Glenn L. Bowers, executive director of the Pennsylvania Game Commission.

Some of the material on the osprey and Hawk Mountain's daily hawk counts draws on two earlier articles of mine: "Behold the Osprey, Before It's Too Late," *Potomac Magazine*, April 23, 1972; and "Assessing the Hawk Counts at Hawk

Mountain," *Proceedings of the North American Osprey Conference*, in press; Alex Nagy, co-author. I thank Alex and the editors of both publications.

Dr. Hickey, Dr. Sutton, Alex Nagy, Jim Brett, Lou Witkin, Dave Titus, Dick Plunkett, and Joseph W. Taylor read part or all of the manuscript and made valuable comments. Good editors are a boon to any book, and Norman Kotker of Scribners stands as gentle godfather and shepherd to this one.

My wife, Mary Durant, while writing her own work, also served as invaluable listener, reader, editor, and critic, all of which lightened the burdens and sharpened the perceptions of the author—who, profoundly grateful to each of the above, wishes to absolve them all from any responsibility for defects in the final product.

M.H.
WASHINGTON, CONNECTICUT
October 22, 1972

The View from Hawk Mountain

ONE

The first hawk of the day appears, soundlessly, rising out of the trees below us this fine, mid-September morning. The time is not yet nine o'clock daylight-saving time —eight o'clock *bird time* as we say, or standard time. The day is warm, the fog is burning out of the valleys, and obviously the air has begun to rise a little, stirring the hawk's impulse to get moving south. It flaps once or twice, then stretches its rounded wings flat into a plane about three feet from tip to tip, and turns slowly in a small circle, feeling for the buoyant air that will lift it. The bird's back and wings are brown, with a touch of olive; the short tail is barred with wide black and white stripes.

"*There's* a broadwing," says one of my companions on North Lookout. This is a weekday, but already there are six of us sitting here on favored boulders, facing east along the spine of the Kittatinny ridge.

"He isn't getting much lift yet."

As it circles below us, the broad-winged hawk manages the air with slight adjustments of its tail and wing feathers. It spreads the tail and the primaries—the first 10 feathers at the back edge of each wing, from the wing tip in; spreads them wide to catch the air, closes a few, twists them for control as it turns, draws all together as it side-slips, spreads the feathers again, circles, flaps once, twice, three times for more altitude, circles—not yet at eye level, feathers twisting, flaring, narrowing, flicking. It is unbelievable that any creature should have such delicate control over so many of its parts. To describe what man does in his winged machines as "flying" is more than generous; compared to the hawk, man just bangs the air, slams through it.

"Well, buddy, where are your brethren?"—addressed to the hawk.

"It's early yet."

"Oh-oh, there they are: one, two, three, four—see, Charlie, under the Hunters' Field."

"Right. I've got another bunch over here, to the left of that."

Someone else finds a third group, then a fourth. Broadwings that set down on the ridge at the end of yesterday's flight are now getting up from perches all over the slopes below us, circling for altitude, seeking the updrafts, ganging up into the groups in which they will travel. This looks to be a good day at Hawk Mountain.

The Kittatinny ridge rises in New York State and, virtually unbroken, marches across northern New Jersey and eastern Pennsylvania all the way to the Maryland border. The Indians gave the ridge its name; Kittatinny means "endless mountain." There are some short outrider ridges between this ridge and the distant sea, but the Kittatinny is essentially the southeast edge of the Appalachian chain.

When the hawks leave their breeding territories in eastern Canada and the northeastern states and move toward the south in the fall—some to winter in New England, some to stop in the Middle Atlantic states, some to go on, even as far as South America—many of them make for the Atlantic coastline and follow that. But large numbers, particularly of the hawks that like to soar, stay inland and follow the Appalachians. The heat rising and the wind rebounding off the mountains provides lift—sheets of rising air, row upon row of combers in the sky—on which they can ride and so cover long distances with relatively little effort.

If the weather is right and the lift is good, they cling to a ridge even when it bends due west. If there's a long break in the ridge or an interrupting jumble of cross-ridges, the hawks look to the south for something better, tack that way to the new air, and ride those currents until something farther south attracts them away. So, striking the Appalachians to the west and north and east, they drop south, ridge to ridge. Sometimes the weather conditions and the topography combine to create a flow directly southward, across the grain of the mountains, and they drift with it, without tacking. The Kittatinny is the last of the great ridges they reach. Beyond it is the Great Valley, the beginning of the lowlands that end at the sea. When the hawks reach the endless mountain, a good many of them stay with it. On some days they pile up along the ridge by the thousands.

Not quite halfway along its course through eastern Pennsylvania—where it is called Blue Mountain for its entire length—the Kittatinny bends west, then south-west, then west again; begins to dip gradually, narrows into a hogback that grows progressively sharper for two miles. Suddenly it rises steeply to a field of sandstone boulders, a field that from the air has the shape of an arrow-head. Just there, the ridge twists abruptly, almost doubling back on itself, and after several miles of zigzagging toward the southeast finally does send out a long spur back toward the northeast as it turns and resumes its southwesterly course. On the inside of the ragged bowl thus created, the flanks of the ridge and its headlands are steep; in places, sandstone cliffs jut out through the trees. The bowl and the stone outcroppings form an amphitheater that looks out on a spectacular migration.

The boulder field shaped like an arrowhead points southwest. In the old days, there was irony in that topo-graphic whimsy: every fall, thousands of migrating birds of prey got no farther southwest than the pointing arrow. Gunners posted themselves there and on the other stone outcroppings, and shot at the passing birds. Broadwings and redtails and red-shoulders and roughlegs and golden eagles and bald eagles and sharpshins and Cooper's hawks and goshawks and peregrines and merlins and kestrels and harriers and ospreys fell dead, or maimed—in the end, the same—into the tops of the red and golden trees, tumbled limply from branch to branch, struck the stony woods' floor. After a day of strong winds from the north or northwest, winds that crowded the birds close against the narrow ridge, the hawks lay in piles beneath the shooting stands.

It is forty years since that last happened here, on what has come to be called Hawk Mountain. Hawkwatchers, not gunners, roost in the arrow-shaped field of boulders —now the North Lookout of Hawk Mountain Sanctuary—and on the other outcroppings, all looking to the east, into the line of flight.

So here I am, once again nestled down on a soft rock, as they say here, with the boulder field dipping gradually down in front of me. There's a big-toothed aspen near the center of the lookout, a tree kept small by the weather; off to one side is a clump of mountain laurel and rhododendron and a mountain ash that bears bright red berries in the fall. All around the front and sides of the lookout are the tops of hemlocks, their roots on the slopes below, and at the back, birches, oaks, black gums, maples, mountain holly, witch hazel, and shoots of American chestnut.

This is my first visit here of the fall hawk-migration season. Between now and the end of November, I will make two or three such visits, as I do each fall I can, driving west from my home in Connecticut and either camping out in one of the Appalachian shelters on the sanctuary or, in November, when the cold at night is more than I care to suffer, denning in with friends.

It is a long way to go to look at birds—a half-day's drive each way. But others regularly come from farther away—Ohio, Georgia, Canada. And, anyway, to me Hawk Mountain is much more than a place to look at birds. To be sure, when I first came here, birds were the attraction. At the time, I was stuck in New York City; perhaps as a reaction to the city, I was becoming interested in birds and in the process beginning to grope and stumble toward finding what I wanted to do in life. Spring and fall mornings, friends and I collected in Central Park on our way to jobs, looking for rarities among the hordes of migrating birds that stop to rest in the park after a long night's flight; weekends, we took trips out of the city, chasing birds. One of my friends knew Hawk Mountain and touted it. My experience with hawks was then practically zero, and I was at the stage in birding that when I focused in on a new bird for my Life List my hands shook with excitement. So we drove down one fall weekend— visions of eagles and goshawks and Cooper's hawks and peregrines dancing in my head. We saw a lot less than I had hoped, and a lot of the hawks we did see I couldn't identify, but the promise of good new birds remained tantalizing. More than that, the feeling these passing birds gave me—that I was somehow at the very heart of the migration—was something I had never experienced anywhere else. Most migration seems to take place almost by magic. You don't see it happening, partly because so much of it goes on at night; suddenly one morning the city park or the front lawn is swarming with robins or towhees or white-throated sparrows. But at Hawk Mountain the flow of southing birds is visible; it goes on and on during a good day, giving an inkling of the breadth and depth of the movement.

My trips to the mountain became an annual ritual. In the next several years, my explorations after birds at Hawk Mountain and elsewhere led me—as if I had been headed that way all the time—into the much larger arena of the world's environment. One cannot spend much time looking for wildlife in the urban Northeast without becoming sensitized to the pressures man is putting on the space in which he lives. I began writing about it. My attitude toward birding changed; I narrowed my focus and spent less and less time trying to add new birds to my Life List. To be sure, I still like to find new birds, and I cannot deny that I still quiver a bit when that happens. But it is clear to me that there are great gaps in man's knowledge about birds, as there are great gaps in his knowledge of the working of all nature and his place in it. That problem attracts me.

Hawk Mountain is engaged, in part, in filling a few of those gaps. For forty years, it has been the only place in the Northeast where the migration of the birds of prey has been observed on a daily basis throughout the fall. Almost since the beginning of the sanctuary's existence, counts of the passing hawks have been made, to develop a picture of the mechanics and timing of the migration, and to give some very rough clues to the numbers and make-up of the northeastern hawk population. The effort is one the experienced amateur can participate in. In fact, because the paid staff of Hawk Mountain Sanctuary is so small, it has to depend on those amateurs to do a great deal of the counting, and to help out around the place in other ways. So when I come to Hawk Mountain in the fall, I come to help with the count and, generally, to take an active role in a valuable environmental venture, as well as to place myself in the dramatic landscape, and in the middle of the passage south of the birds of prey.

Down to the right of North Lookout, along the first southeastward bend of the Hawk Mountain zigzag, are four outcroppings of stone. The farthest away, about half a mile off, is South Lookout. Both North and South will be manned today, sharing the job of counting. The two lookouts are connected by walkie-talkies, so as to prevent double counting and to allow us to keep each other apprised of approaching birds.

If you work your way east from here, up the ridge about a quarter of a mile—climbing over monstrous rocks as you go—and then look across at South Lookout, you see that it stands at the top of a long slide of rock, with huge boulders at the base, several hundred feet down. The middle of the valley, which is called the Kettle, is filled with these boulders—some of them as big as freight cars. The forest has grown up and covered most of this rock pile, but in the center it is still bare in patches, and the patches are strung out in such a way that together they have the name, River of Rocks. The distance between the observer on the heights and the boulder fields in the valley is so great, perspective is lost. The awesome size and roughness of the boulders is unexpected, and the new visitor invariably asks if that is a dry stream-bed—a gentle image of stones worn smooth and round by flowing water, not behemoths shed by the mountain in its age. A small stream—Kettle Creek—does run under the River of Rocks, and rises to the surface beyond it, in a great tangle of rhododendron; in the spring runoff, the creek and the brooklets that feed it from above rise high enough to wash away most of the soil that has collected between the great boulders, but that is the only time the stream and the rocks are joined. Maurice Broun, the first curator of the sanctuary, called it "the upside-down river."

These ridges of the Appalachian chain, once the bottom of an ocean, were anciently formed by a folding and thrusting up of the earth's crust. They wore down and were thrust up again, and now they are being worn down once more—by wind and rain and the ice of winter that, as it freezes, shoves boulders from their places and splits off chunks of stone. During each winter, the lookouts change their shapes. ("My rock seems to have moved a bit," said one veteran watcher as she settled onto a favorite seat early in September.)

I have put a pillow between me and the sandstone. Twice in the past I've gone through a pair of pants on these rocks, from not bringing some sort of cushion, or not using it once I'd brought it. The regulars carry their pillows under their arms or in knapsacks with their lunches, pillows of great variety—slabs of foam rubber, air chairs, ancient army blankets, ponchos, throw pillows carefully recovered with sturdy canvas and sometimes embroidered with the owner's name. A few old-timers arrive on North Lookout wearing their pillows like reverse aprons tied around the waist, so that when they move from rock to rock their pillows stay with them. Necessity is the mother of invention.

One is always conscious of the stoniness of this territory—in the old days, truly a wealth of rock. Sand was once mined on Hawk Mountain, and the remains of the quarry, an overhang of crumbling sandstone, stand not far from North Lookout. "A lot of our Pennsylvania Dutch homesteads around here are made out of this mountain stone," Alex Nagy, the present curator, told me recently. "It's called Tuscarora quartzite, Tuscarora sandstone, Blue Mountain stone, or bacon stone—because of the lines of red running through it. You break it open, and nine times out of ten you'll find the red pigmentation in there, due to the iron compound."

Slate, too, was mined in the area. "All along the mountain here," Alex said, "the shale has been metamorphosed into slate, and some places it's very close to the surface. Many farms have their little shale pits, and on the south side of the ridge there are places called Slateville and Slatedale and Slatington." There was some marble quarrying, too, and copper mining. The iron mines were the source of an important industry just south of the mountain; Bethlehem and Reading in particular came into their own because of it. There is also the coal, of course, although by now coal mining has almost stopped hereabouts. It used to be said of this region that most of its railroad network was underground—miles and miles of track following tunnels back to the coal veins being worked. North of Hawk Mountain, toward Hazleton and Scranton, the landscape is horribly scarred and desolate with the gouges and tailings of abandoned strip mines. A little coal is still being dug in the vicinity, within earshot of the sanctuary; the distant thud of dynamite blasting can be heard on the lookouts.

South Lookout and the River of Rocks are just two of the landmarks in the view. Hawkwatchers use these landmarks to locate approaching birds for each other. Beyond and below the South Lookout headland, the roof of Headquarters rises among the trees. The old two-story building, which dates from the American Revolution and is called Schaumboch's by the old-timers, sits against the winding state road that connects the village of Eckville, in Berks County, on one side of the mountain, with the village of Drehersville, in Schuylkill County, on the other side. (Around Headquarters, but out of sight from here, is a loose cluster of buildings: the Common Room, where hawkwatchers collect on rainy days and for the lecture series, Saturday nights; the curator's house; two Appalachian shelters for campers; and several sheds and outhouses.) Farther to the southeast, more than two miles away, a headland drops to the valley—Owl's Head. There is another lookout there, around the corner and hidden from the two main lookouts. In the distance behind Owl's Head, a promontory called the Pinnacle reaches its long spur, parallel to the main stem of the ridge, out into the valley. Crossing the valley now, headed back toward the ridge, the villages of Eckville and Wanamakers. Beyond is a strange-looking mound called the Donat, which seems to rise high out of the flat plain like some huge Indian burial mound; the name is often corrupted to Donut, but Donat it is, named for a family that once owned property there. Donats still live in the area, though not on the hill any longer. In the distance beyond it, when the day is crystal clear, one can see Allentown and Bethlehem, with the help of binoculars, but southwesterly days like this one are usually too hazy. Now the ridge, winding back to the northeast: from the vantage point of North Lookout, the bends and folds in the ridge produce five gentle peaks, the nearest, on the left, two miles away, the farthest, on the right, four miles, and these peaks have been numbered, one to five; but for some reason now long forgotten, they were numbered backwards in the beginning, from right to left—an ornithological folk tradition, very confusing to the newcomer. He may recognize the intent of a number in someone's direction, "Broadwing off the slope of One," but almost always he will look toward the wrong side of the ridge—and at empty sky, most likely. After doing that a few times, he will mutter something to the effect that *he* can't see anything out there, Goddammit, and then maybe someone will check where he is aiming the binoculars and correct the misapprehension.

The views to the east are long, but confined within headlands and valleys. To the north of the ridge they open up; looking that way, one sits at the edge of a huge 180-degree panorama. The mountainside drops precipitously, about a thousand feet, from the edge of North Lookout, down into a long valley of farms and villages that spreads several miles to the next ridge—Second Mountain; the name reminds one how great a barrier the Appalachians were to the early settlers. Beyond Second Mountain, Sharp Mountain, then Broad Mountain; they march in what looks almost like neat ranks, one horizon behind the other, some 25 miles to the northwest.

There are landmarks in that view, too: the villages of Orwigsburg and McKeansburg and New Ringgold; the tracks of the Reading Rail Road and the Little Schuylkill River, curving together, far below, around the foot of the mountain; an automobile graveyard near New Ringgold, referred to from here as the Junkyard; dozens of clusters of farm buildings; Christmas tree plantations, cornfields, and pastures, including one where bow hunters camped years ago, which has ever since been called, on North Lookout, the Hunters' Field.

The prospect from this mountaintop is tremendous. Views 20 or 30 miles long stretch out to an arc of horizon 70 miles around. I used not to appreciate it much. I have never been comfortable with heights, and when, on my first visit to the sanctuary, having trudged up the two-thirds of a mile through the woods and followed the arrows and blazes painted on rocks until I was out in the open, I found myself on the brink of a ledge, looking out across the broad valley to the north, with the world a quarter of a mile almost straight down, I felt as if I had lost the better part of my specific gravity. I picked my way, trembling, ev-er so care-fully, down off the ledge and into the middle of the field of boulders, chose a rock to sit on and tried to make an anchor of it, ballast my fear with it. And every autumn since, when I have made my first climb to North Lookout, I have felt echoing twinges. But, despite that, I now walk down onto the lookout and take in the view and feel I have come home.

Wherever I am, when the wind is in the northwest and the air has a bite to it, the view from Hawk Mountain spreads itself before me in my memory and I long to be a part of it—the ancient upthrust mountains, the enormous space, the rhythms of weather, the passing of birds that are the essence of wildness, all speaking of measures of time that dwarf man.

Early one morning Alex Nagy, a hefty, amiable man with a black mustache and thick black hair brushed straight back, drove two of us volunteer hawk counters out toward the lookout at Owl's Head. As usual, his white German shepherd, Snowball, stood in the back of the pickup, her head over the side and tongue out, managing to stay upright despite the roughness of the narrow track. Alex drove slowly, keeping an eye peeled for wild turkey and deer.

Alex's father, who has a farm below the sanctuary, near Eckville, is Hungarian, and Alex credits this origin, in an indirect way, for his own gravitating toward conservation work. "Where he came from, in Hungary, they had to learn all the flowers and all the birds and all the animals of the country. He said they learned that in kindergarten, right through. Here, you don't get any of that.

"Let me tell you, I was absolutely amazed—one day, I was down at the farm, and this was during the Hungarian purge, when all the freedom fighters came over, this young boy about twelve years old came out of the house. He was just starting to speak English, and we were out looking at birds, and, boy, he was telling me about how this particular sparrow looked like a certain bird in his country. I asked him, 'Gee, how come you know so much about it?' And he told me the exact same thing my dad did.

"What's the point in knowing that Bolivia exports tin when you can't even tell a barn owl in your back yard? They're both important, but I think you really ought to know all the outdoor furniture you have around. So it's a whole different attitude they have." From the time he was small, his father took him on walks in the woods and taught him the outdoor furniture.

The elder Nagy had come here as a boy and had started working in the local iron and steel industry in his teens, hauling water for the mules in a quarry where limestone was mined for building blast furnaces; he eventually became a department superintendent, before he "retired" and took up farming. Alex also had his first summer job in a steel mill. "My father thought he'd let me start from the bottom and work my way up, but I started *underground*, actually, because I used to work in the scale pits underneath the rolling mills. We used to have 48-inch ingots going through there, y'know, and all that scale would fly down into the pits underneath. Well, they shut the machinery down, just for a few minutes, it seemed, and you'd go in there with wooden clogs on the bottom of your feet, and it's all *hot*—hell can't be any worse than that, because it's dusty, hot, and some of the scale is still practically red-hot, y'know. So you shovel all this stuff into the buckets and haul it out, and, of course, they quick start rolling steel again, to keep up production."

Alex graduated from high school, and when the Second World War came along he was hustled through a speed-up course at the Merchant Marine Academy, graduating as an engineer. He spent the war sailing on merchant ships in the Mediterranean, and came back to Berks County to help his father on the farm for a while. As a neighbor of the sanctuary, he became a Hawk Mountain regular, and occasionally helped with chores on the sanctuary. One day (he was married now, and he had a job as engineer in the Bethlehem Steel power house), he paid a visit, and found Maurice Broun out working along the road. The curator said he was looking for an assistant, and asked Alex if he knew anyone who might be interested.

" 'Well,' I said, 'how about *me?*' " Alex laughed as he told the story. "Just like that, you know. I wasn't even living in the area at the time. I used to come up in the fall and watch the hawks and spend time here. And, really, I didn't even ask Arlene or give it much thought or anything. I just kind of blurted it out."

He was hired, and he took over responsibility for physical care of the sanctuary, greeted weekend visitors at the entrance, and helped with the hawk counts. Cheerful, patient, enthusiastic, he became a fixture here, and when Maurice Broun retired, Alex was the obvious choice as successor. He had no formal training in ornithology or, for that matter, in any of the natural sciences, but he had been steeped in it when young, and Hawk Mountain itself provided the higher education. He, too, had come home.

I arrived at Hawk Mountain this fall in time for the peak of the broadwing migration, one of the greatest spectacles of the season. On our way out to Owl's Head in Alex's pickup, a large brown bird started from its perch in a tree ahead of us, flew about 50 yards, and swooped up to a new perch on a branch over the road. "Oh-ho," said Alex, "a broadwing." He put the pickup in low gear, and we crept toward the bird. It is an indication of the excitement stirred in us by hawks that we would pause in this way to study a single individual of a species we were likely to see hundreds, perhaps thousands of that day. The bird waited until we were 15 yards off, then dropped from the branch and flew ahead of us to another perch. As we approached it again, I remarked that it didn't seem very concerned about us. "Oh, sure," Alex said, "sometimes I drive out here and broadwings will do this for almost two miles— all the way to Owl's Head." Our bird, as it turned out, stayed with us for only a hundred yards more, then tired of the game and flapped away through the woods.

In the breeding season, the broadwing nests in woods from northern Florida up into Canada and west to the Canadian Rockies. It likes to have openings near its nest —meadows, or trails, and preferably a pond or brook, too. Because it doesn't start away noisily with great flap-pings and squawkings when you get close to it in the woods, it is very easily overlooked. The bird sits on a branch, head down into its shoulders and maybe its wings drooping a bit, and watches the intruder pass, possibly right underneath. Often, I don't notice a broadwing until I hear it cry—usually a mournful, suppressed scream, *p'deeeeee*—and even then the source is hard to track down if the bird sits tight, because it seems to be able to throw its voice.

Courting pairs of broadwings soar low above the forest or along its edge, call to each other, slowly circle side by side, peel off, crying, and head in opposite directions, loop back to cross paths, separate and drop into the tops of the trees to sit silently, until one—probably the male—is stirred again, flaps out into the open, and calls its mate to join it.

Having arrived in the Northeast from Central and South American winter homes at the middle or end of April, a broadwing pair builds a nest in the main crotch of a tree or at the joint of the trunk and a branch, breeds in May or June, raises two or three young, and then all start south again in August or September.

To some observers, the broadwing is disappointingly unhawklike—slow-moving, quiet, relatively gentle, with quite unmajestic tastes in food. It eats insects, snakes, earthworms, frogs, toads, crayfish, some small birds and mammals, even fish occasionally. In 1925, William Brewster of Massachusetts—who tended to moralize on the habits of birds—commented sourly about the toad eating: "It seems to prefer these unattractive batrachians to any other prey, perhaps because they are so easily secured; for at all times when not diverting itself by aerial flights the Broadwing is one of the most sluggish and indolent of birds, rarely undertaking any vigorous exertion which can well be avoided. Of this its predilection for toad-hunting and manner of pursuing it afford evidence no less amusing than convincing. After alighting on a low branch or stub overlooking some shallow reach of calm water besprinkled with innumerable floating toads absorbed in the cares and pleasures of procreation, . . . the Hawk will often gaze down at them long and listlessly, as if undecided which particular one to select from among so many, or dreamily gloat over the wealth of opportunities. . . . It may finally glide swiftly, yet without effort, along a slight downward incline to a toad forty or fifty yards away, or may drop more abruptly and awkwardly on one closer at hand, flapping its wings at the last moment to check the impetus of its descent."

Audubon had a somewhat similar impression of the broadwing's character. He and his young brother-in-law William Blakewell were on a May walk in Pennsylvania when William spotted a bird on a nest and climbed the tree, to try to see what it was when it flew and then to relieve it of one of its eggs. But it wouldn't fly. So William wrapped the unprotesting bird—which he recognized as some kind of hawk—in a handkerchief and managed to get it and its eggs to the ground in good order. Audubon was delighted. He had never seen this species, which he called the broad-winged buzzard. However, he "felt vexed," he wrote, "that it was not of a more spirited nature, as it had neither defended its eggs nor itself." He brought it home to the inlaws', where he had a studio.

"I put the bird on a stick made fast to my table. It merely moved its feet to grasp the stick, and stood erect, but raised its feathers, and drew in its neck on its shoulders. I passed my hand over it, to smooth the feathers. . . . It moved not. The plumage remained as I wished it. Its eye, directed toward mine, appeared truly sorrowful. I measured the length of its bill with the compass, began my outlines, continued measuring part after part as I went on, and finished the drawing, without the bird ever moving once." He evidently liked the result; in the Audubon engraving eventually done of the species, the female is this very bird. Now finished, the artist opened a window, carried the hawk to it and let it go; ". . . it sailed off until out of my sight, without uttering a single cry, or deviating from its course."

There have been many seconds to this impression of mildness in the broadwing's personality. But it is a contradictory bird. B. H. Warren, a medical doctor who served as ornithologist for the Pennsylvania Board of Agriculture at the end of the last century and wrote a detailed *Report on the Birds of Pennsylvania*, remarked that he, too, had "always found it to be cowardly, and to evince no disposition to repel an invasion of its nest." However, he said, it would seem "that the disposition of this bird . . . is very variable. . . . A man . . . employed to obtain a nest, was attacked with great fury, while ascending the tree; his cap was torn from his head, and he would have been seriously injured if the bird had not been shot." Another broadwing, he added, flew at a boy who was climbing the nest tree, "fastened her talons in his arm, and could not be removed until beaten off and killed with a club." I mentioned the supposed tameness to a falconer once, and he raised his eyebrows. "Don't you believe it," he said. "I've been attacked at the nest, and they are *mean*."

Perhaps such variations in behavior are to be expected in a bird as numerous as the broadwing. At Hawk Mountain, as at all the inland hawkwatches in the Northeast, fourteen kinds of hawks are regularly seen in the fall, but usually at least one-third of the total number of passing hawks, and sometimes more than two-thirds, are broadwings. One year, 18,507 of them were counted at Hawk Mountain, and Hawk Mountain is by no means the premier hawk watch as far as broadwings are concerned. There are places along the northern shore of the Great Lakes where one can see 18,000 migrating broadwings in a single day—and still be a little disappointed, because there was one September day in 1961 when more than 70,000 of these birds passed Hawk Cliffs, a hawk watch on Lake Erie. Those 70, 000 probably represented only a fraction of the broadwings —even just of those from Canada.

The figures are nothing as impressive as the sight itself. The broadwings rise from their overnight roosts, circle to gain altitude—as they are doing this morning. Being members of the Buteo family, hawks built for soaring, with wings quite broad, long, and rounded, and with short, wide tails, they seek out thermals that will lift them. These thermals develop as the ground gets warm—bubbles of heat that, rising, form doughnut-shaped rings of warm air. Air is sucked into a ring of heat from below, rises, cools, and then falls out beyond the circumference of the ring. On a warm day with a light wind, there are thermals rising all over the map, some better than others. The broadwings, like most migrating hawks, have an eye out for the best updrafts; apparently, if one broadwing is rising faster than another, the second hawk will leave its thermal and join the more favored bird. Gradually they begin to collect in large groups—dozens, hundreds, sometimes thousands —and they swirl upward on the thermals in a mixing and crisscrossing of individual spirals that give such flocks the nickname "kettle" or "boil." Eventually the uppermost birds leave the elevator and "set": the wing and tail feathers that have been fanned wide to catch the lift now shut tight; each hawk hunches its shoulders, shortening its wingspan to reduce drag even more, and, using gravity, starts to coast toward the next thermal. One after another, the rest of the kettle follows suit, and the hawks string out against the sky, dark shapes, like drawn crossbows, streaking downhill.

That's the classic pattern, seen on the warm days with

light winds. Under different conditions, the broadwings may proceed differently. A good strong wind out of the northwest may induce them to kettle less often and, instead, get down close to the windward side of the ridge until they are riding the crests of the waves of air rebounding from the slope—the wind supporting them and blowing them southwestward at the same time. Or, on a northerly day, they may get well up into the wind and just drift south, high overhead. How they move on any given day —what paths they follow, how high they fly, how many of them are migrating—is not yet understood at all well. They don't seem to obey the same rules as the other hawks.

"There are really two migrations," Alex Nagy says. "There's the broadwings, and then there's all the other hawks." For instance, fog is not thought to be very encouraging to migrating hawks, but one year the broadwings passed Hawk Mountain in what were apparently large numbers, during a week when fog clung to the top of the ridge much of the time. Watchers on North Lookout, completely socked in and waiting impatiently for the weather to clear, would suddenly see 50 or 60 birds at a time swirl out of a break in the fog a hundred feet away and then vanish again.

Birds of prey normally refuse to fly in rain, but on at least one day in recent memory, a major movement of broadwings took place in a light drizzle. Winds from the north-to-west quadrant of the compass generally produce the best counts of hawks at Hawk Mountain, but the big broadwing days are just as likely to come when the wind is in the east. A wind of some kind is considered the *sine qua non* of hawk migration—"No wind, no hawks," Maurice Broun used to say—but thousands of broadwings may pass here on a day of flat calm. Maurice himself wrote of a bewildering series of events: five days of supposedly fine migrating weather in the middle of the 1948 broadwing season, in which only 1,500 of them were counted, followed by a day that began with an easterly wind and ended absolutely airless, during which day more than 11,000 broadwings passed. Seventy-five hundred of them were counted in the last hour of that morning, and at times there were simply too many in view to count, and the numbers had to be estimated. Maurice declared himself utterly perplexed as to why this happened. Aaron Bagg of Massachusetts, who was for years one of the most active birders in the Northeast, was counting hawks that same day in his home state. He noted that "winds of a northerly or northeasterly character prevailed over almost the entire region from which Hawk Mountain . . . might expect to receive migrants." Broadwings are relatively light in relation to the size of their wings, and so they tend to be more at the mercy of the wind than other Buteos. Possibly that had something to do with it, the northerly and northeasterly winds pushing the birds toward the mountain. But no one knows. In short, broadwings are unpredictable.

A good deal of predicting about their passage goes on, nonetheless. It is one of the favorite pastimes of hawk-watchers. The flight of broadwings starts early in August, builds to a peak in September, and tails off quickly after that; big kettles of broadwings are seldom seen in Pennsylvania in October. Aficionados like myself try to time our arrivals at Hawk Mountain so that we get there when the daily counts are rising but are not yet very impressive, thus giving us a good shot at being on hand for the Big Day. Judging by the sanctuary's records, that day can come any time between the eleventh and the twenty-fourth of September. To guess which will be the day, the hawkwatcher follows the weather maps: a rule of thumb is that once a low pressure area has passed over the Great Lakes or New England, with a cold front behind it to give the birds a shove, then within a day or two the migration watching will be excellent at Hawk Mountain. Since that isn't always the key to the Big Day, however, you also try to feel it in your bones, sniff it in the air, and influence the birds by extrasensory thought transference. And when you reach the top of the mountain in the morning, with the mist lifting from the valleys and the sun burning through, you greet the watchers who are already in place with the incantation, "Well, today's the day."

This morning, there is a thermal rising just in front of the lookout, and the early broadwings collect there, swirl up over us—every barb in every wing and tail feather illuminated for us by the sun behind them. Twenty, 30, 40 of them at a time—adults with the wide-barred tails and the cinnamon breasts, birds of the year with thinly striped brown tails and brown-streaked underparts—the Compleat Broadwing. When the third kettle of the day is overhead, we become aware of odd behavior. The two dozen soaring shapes thrust out legs; tails and wings contract suddenly, then erect, as the birds slide and brake quickly, snatching at something. They bend their heads to raised claws, and eat. Evidently, large insects are swarming above the lookout, possibly migrating dragonflies, although no one can tell for sure. For the next hour or so, every kettle that passes does the same thing; sometimes practically all the birds in a kettle display the unexpected angularities at once—the gliding flight hyphenated by short lunges and swoops.

By eleven o'clock, North and South Lookouts have

counted between them more than 900 broadwings, plus a scattering of other hawks. Not bad, but this evidently isn't The Day after all. We should have seen a couple of thousand broadwings by now. As usual on such a warm and hazy day, with good thermals building up, the flight paths of the birds have risen higher and higher as the morning wore on, until many of the hawks are invisible to the naked eye and have shrunk to spots in the binoculars. At eleven, the flight seems to stop completely. Not a single bird is visible. This is a common phenomenon, referred to as the midday lull. Hawkwatchers debate endlessly about where the birds go during a lull. There's no reason to think they have stopped flying, settled into the trees for a siesta, or come down to hunt for food. Perhaps they have simply risen too high—two or three miles above us—to be seen even in the binoculars. Or it may be that in the early morning, as the thermals rise from the ridges, which are first to feel the sun, the hawks start by following the spine of the Kittatinny, but that by midday the valleys, more or less free of cooling foliage, have warmed up so that they are producing the better thermals, and the hawks are now not only very high but are following flight paths well away from the ridge. Again, no one knows. Some days there is no lull. Some early afternoons, when the thermals rising from the valley should be at their strongest, the lull ends and the broadwings appear again along the ridge. A mystery.

We break out lunches, enjoy the view, and chat. Monarch butterflies, themselves headed south and using the Kittatinny air currents for lift, float across the lookout. Yellow jackets buzz around the sandwiches and thermoses, and at the top of the lookout, the volunteer who is responsible today for taking the count on North Lookout drops pieces of his sandwich at the mouth of a hole between rocks; a tiny red-backed vole scurries out and eats. Migrating warblers in their drab fall plumage browse for insects among the laurels and in the treetops on the slopes below us, and a couple of times some of us leap from rock to rock to look down at a Cape May warbler or at a resident pileated woodpecker—red-crested and big as a crow—as it flies, screaming triumphantly, to one of the big larders of carpenter ants it has dug out in a dead tree. But most birds that are not hawks, to a hawkwatcher on a lookout, are of secondary interest and are referred to as mere "dickey-birds," "tweety-birds," even—with a grin—as "hawk food." We continue to sweep the horizon with our binoculars. We are like fishermen when the fish stop biting—occasionally checking to see if the quarry has returned, but prepared for a long wait. Some of us try magic to change our luck. A birder leaving for a trip to the outhouses halfway down the trail announces that he is making "the supreme sacrifice," and there is general agreement that as soon as he departs the hawks will start flying. I have a flask of brandy in my pack, against the chill of the coming evening, and I offer to pass it around if someone spots an eagle.

But the wait this day is unusually long. The wind dies. In the four hours between eleven and three, not a single hawk passes either North or South Lookout. Now people have begun to stir from their rocks, pack up their gear, and head down the mountain; this late, after such an empty spell, not much is likely to happen. "You're going to miss the three o'clock eagle," a die-hard says to one of them —it's a standing joke—and the departing watcher grins and shakes her head.

Just before three, the radio on North Lookout makes its

furry introductory noise—a send button being pushed. But instead of a voice, the strains of a recorded funeral dirge sound tinnily through the speaker; someone on South Lookout has evidently come prepared for such a day as this. We burst out laughing, while Barbara Lake, the chipper, alert secretary of the sanctuary staff, comes on the air from Headquarters to remind us that the Hawk Mountain broadcasting license does not permit the sending of music.

But it breaks the spell. A few minutes later, a small kettle of broadwings and one marsh hawk, its wings set in a long, shallow V, appears off the slope of One; the hawks circle up, set, and head our way. Putting my binoculars back on the spot where they appeared, I find another small kettle spiraling over the ridge, with one large bird standing out among the broadwings. The big bird looks to me like an osprey—dark-backed hunter of fish—and I call it out; others on the lookout find the bird, and there is general agreement. However, our count taker has trouble picking it up, though he is aiming his glasses in the right direction, and when he finally does, he says almost immediately, "Oh, yeah? *That's* no osprey."

"Does it have a white head?" someone asks hopefully.

"That's what it looks like to me. Bald eagle. Hot dog!" And he reaches for the handset. "KJB211, North Lookout to South, over."

"South Lookout."

"We have an adult bald eagle, low on the slope of One. Should be about over the Burn for you." The Burn is a fire scar on the flank of the ridge; it's a landmark for South, though we can't see it from here.

"We've been watching him," says our friend on the

radio, making no attempt to hide a tone of one-upness, "but thank you."

The eagle comes at us quite fast, well below eye level, rowing steadily along the ridge, then turns and angles down to pass between the two lookouts. The sun at our backs has the valley in shadow by now, but the diffuse, reflected light cast on the bird's white head and tail is perfect. The watchers who have stuck it out these four hours are exultant; that was worth the wait.

The eagle beats his way up and over the bend in the ridge behind us, and the sky is once more empty. After 15 minutes, I remember my offer of brandy, and the pewter flask is ceremoniously handed around, in honor of the eagle. The count taker cocks his white cowboy hat down over his eyes and stretches out against a rock, as if accepting the fact that now the day's flight is over. At four, he rouses himself to make out his hourly report on the tally sheet and call in the figures to Headquarters—19 broadwings, a marsh hawk, and a bald eagle; South Lookout does the same, adding a few more broadwings, another marsh hawk, and a goshawk. This should have been a great day for broadwings, but for some reason it hasn't been. And by now, they should be settling down for the night.

A few minutes after four, one of the watchers, scanning the sky, aims his binoculars over the broad valley to the north and shouts in astonishment. There is a huge boil of birds out there; already some of the hawks have set, are past us, and are streaking toward the west. The count taker sits up, snatches his binoculars to his eyes with one hand, takes his mechanical counter in the other and starts pressing the plunger rapidly, registering some 300 broadwings in the next five minutes—all well out over the valley. As the last of them glide past, I track back along the path they followed until I am looking at the ridge. Just above it, between knobs Five and Four, is another kettle. Even at two miles, I can see there are hundreds and hundreds of birds there—a storm of broadwings. They rise slowly out of the haze, and the leaders do not wait long to set. They start toward us, four, six, ten abreast, and pass directly over our heads. The lead birds are past us, but still over Four and Five hawks are kettling. I pick my way over boulders down to the middle of the lookout, to get a longer view behind us. From the tops of the trees there, back to the crest of the ridge in the east, the column of hawks streams toward the west—two miles of hawks. For several minutes there is no end to them. I find myself standing with my arms spread wide toward the birds.

And then they are gone. In less than 15 minutes, we have seen more than a thousand broadwings.

TWO

The shooting of hawks along the Kittatinny ridge had gone on at least since 1870, probably earlier. Charles Mohl, an old hunter in Drehersville, a man now in his seventies and grown too blind to go gunning for his favorite game —pheasant and grouse—remembers his grandfather saying, "they seen hawks, in the fall of the year, coming down, that it made a shadow when they flew through when the sun was shining." Up at the Sand-head, as they called the high point of the mountain, the sand quarry was operating in those days, just back of and below what is now North Lookout. The sand was quarried out and tracked around in mule-drawn cars through a cut to the head of a narrow-gauge, gravity-operated railway that plunged down the steep north side of the mountain—along what was known as the Slide or Plane—to the sandhouse, a grinding mill in the valley at Drehersville. As one ore car, loaded with rough sand and chunks of stone, was lowered down the Slide, its weight was used to draw up an empty car from the sandhouse; halfway up the Slide, there was a turnout that allowed the two cars to pass each other. Charles Mohl's father and grandfather both worked at the quarry and saw the hawk flights passing overhead each year. "They took a shot at it now and then, but not very often."

There was organized shooting for hawks elsewhere along ridges in those days, and there may well have been a time in the mid-eighties when considerable hawk-gunning went on at the Sand-head, given the local knowledge of those flights. In 1885, the Commonwealth of Pennsylvania passed what came to be called the Scalp Act, offering 50 cents a head for hawks, owls, weasels, and minks. But having paid out some $90,000 in bounties and peace justices' fees for the 128,571 predators killed during the next year and a half, the legislature had second thoughts and repealed the act. Whether or not the mountain was much of a hawk-killing spot then, its heyday was still ahead of it.

Sam Turner's family lived in the little inn called Schaumboch's (pronounced Jumbocks in Sam Turner's heavy Pennsylvania-Dutch accent) near the top of the mountain, on the Eckville side. He was born there in 1900; his family kept the "hotel" open until 1916, when old Mr. Turner died, and six years later they moved away for good. Sam Turner knew the mountain well; he was always out after honeybees and groundhogs and huckleberries, and he dragged lumber—oak and hemlock—down off the summit for part of his living. However much gunning there might have been in the last century, he remembers no hawk shooting there in his day. "That was before my time."

Charles Mohl's recollection was a lot like Sam Turner's. "There was shooting," he said, "but not much. There was a good reason. The people had a shell, they saved it. They didn't want to waste it on a hawk. I know a fella down here, when he went hunting, he wouldn't shoot a rabbit that run out. He waited to find them sitting in the nest, so he was sure he wouldn't miss it. He didn't want to lose that shot."

But after the First World War, wages went up. "And as soon as people started to get a little more money, then they could afford to buy a box of shells now and then."

Most of these men hunted game from the time they were small boys, and most of them had their own guns before they were in their teens. They walked the woods, as did Sam Turner, after rabbits or berries or deer, or just exploring; they learned the territory as if it were all one great big backyard. "I've seen lots of that mountain. Lots of it," said Charles Mohl. "That mountain from there over to close to Hamburg, there wasn't a goddarned road or a big rock or a something that we didn't know where it was." All of them were—and those that survive still are—proud of their knowledge, their skill with a gun, their endurance. Charles Mohl found he was going blind one day when he was shooting rabbits, not so long ago. His dog started a rabbit; he brought his gun up to his left shoulder, couldn't see the rabbit any longer, put the gun down, raised it again and lost the rabbit again. So he came home and set up a target on the barn. Shooting at the target, he found he was three feet off. His left eye was worthless for hunting, and he'd always shot left-handed. So he practiced shooting right-handed, but when he went out in the field again, and a pheasant or a grouse burst from in front of him, he automatically brought the gun to his left shoulder, and by the time he switched over, the bird was gone. Furious, he came home. Since he had always been able to hit grouse and pheasant shooting his shotgun from the hip, he walked around his place with just that in mind, and killed two ring-necked pheasant. Then he quit hunting, for good. Sitting in a lawn chair in front of his house, under an enormous Norway maple he had planted when his family first moved in—about 1900—he remarked that a friend had met him in the barbershop recently, and the friend had said, " 'It always happens. The man with the best eyes get the poorest.' He says, 'A buddy of yours could look a fish in six feet of water like nobody's business, and he got blind. And,' he says, 'you were one of the best grouse shooters around here.' 'Oh,' I says, 'I wouldn't say that.' 'Yes,' he says, 'I *will* say that,' he says, 'and now your eyes are poor.' 'Well,' I says, 'that ain't got nothing to do with my eyes, as far as that's concerned.' "

And seventy-two-year-old Sam Turner, over on the far side of the mountain, "over close to Hamburg," taking care of thousands of acres of Hamburg reservoir property, brags about how badly he was hurt in an accident twenty years ago and how strong he is now (a stout, cagey-looking mountain man in blue coveralls, steel-rimmed spectacles, and old slouch hat), brags about how well he knows the territory and its trails and old roads through the woods, about the numbers of snakes he's killed, the Indian graves he's found, the hundreds of Appalachian Trail hikers that pass through the reservoir property in weekends, and the hundreds of No Trespassing signs he's posted there—not to keep the hikers out, but to give him some leverage if anyone misbehaves. A particular misbehavement is warned against on a few hand-painted signs, one of which reads:

NOTICE

THI. SI. DRINKIN

G. WATER. NO. WAS

HING. FEET. IN.

THIS. CRICK.

Hunting was in their blood, and hunting feeds on traditions. One of those traditions when they were young was that the only good hawk was a dead hawk. Hawks killed poultry and grouse and pheasants and rabbits and songbirds. This was so, in their eyes, despite whatever the Authorities might tell them. Thoughtful conservationists were beginning to realize, well before the turn of this century, that hawks, despite their reputations, often performed a useful service by feeding on pests that damaged crops and preyed heavily on the eggs and young of game birds.

Dr. C. Hart Merriam, chief of the US Biological Survey, attacked the "Scalp Act" in Pennsylvania shortly before its brief life was ended. "Granting that 5,000 chickens are killed annually in Pennsylvania by Hawks and Owls," wrote Dr. Merriam, "and that they are worth twenty-five cents each (a liberal estimate in view of the fact that a large portion of them are killed when very young), the total loss . . . in a year and a half would be . . . $1,875. Hence it appears that during the past eighteen months the State of Pennsylvania has expended $90,000 to save its farmers a loss of $1,875. But this estimate by no means represents the actual loss to the farmer and the taxpayer. . . . It is within bounds to say that within the course of a year every Hawk and Owl destroys at least a thousand mice or their equivalent in insects, and that each mouse or its equivalent so destroyed would cause the loss of two cents per annum. Therefore, omitting all reference to the enormous increase in numbers of these noxious animals when nature's means of holding them in check has been removed, the lowest possible value to the farmer of each Hawk, Owl and Weasel would be . . . $30 in a year and a half.

"Hence," continued Dr. Merriam, "in addition to the $90,000 actually expended by the State in destroying 128,571 of its benefactors, it has incurred a loss to its agricultural interests of at least $3,857,130. . . . In other words, the State has thrown away $2,105 for every dollar saved!"

In 1893, the Department of Agriculture published a book by Dr. A. K. Fisher, *The Hawks and Owls of the United States and Their Relation to Agriculture*. Dr. Fisher had actually taken the trouble to examine the stomach contents of numerous specimens of hawks, eagles, falcons, and owls, and he was able to demonstrate that most birds of prey ate mainly mice and rats and snakes and insects and similar beasts that the farmers and hunters treated as enemies, or ate prey that didn't seem to affect man one way or the other. Reflecting this new awareness, the American Ornithologists' Union eventually suggested a hawk law to the state legislatures. It protected all birds of prey except the great horned owl and the three "blue darters"—the speedy, short-winged and long-tailed forest hawks of the Accipiter family: the Cooper's hawk, the sharp-shinned hawk, and the goshawk. All three Accipiters were admitted to prey heavily on other birds, and the two largest, the Cooper's and the gos, and occasionally even the sharpshin, did make raids on chicken yards. A good many of the states took the advice to some extent, and protected at least some of their birds of prey. In Pennsylvania, the eagles and the osprey and the smallest and prettiest of the American falcons, the kestrel, were taken off the list of fair game.

But that didn't change the minds of many farmers or many hunters. They knew what they knew, and what their fathers had seen and said, too, and *their* fathers before them. Hawks were vermin. "Chicken hawk" or "hen hawk" to them meant just about any hawk at all. Even if you knew about Dr. Fisher's work, and accepted it, or if you knew the state law and could identify the protected hawks—and most hunters couldn't—the invitation to shoot any of the hawks was an invitation to shoot all of them, if only for the fun of it.

Of an evening, early in the 20's, the men would gather in the store beside the Little Schuylkill and the railroad. "That time," remembers Charles Mohl, "there was always 15, 16 fellas there. We didn't have no place to sit down most of the time, unless they had a barl or a nail keg. They had a big bench in there and about six chairs. If there wasn't a dozen men, or say eight there, it was a poor night. . . . Yuh. That's where they met, down at the store, and during the summer, on the porch." They sat around, talking about the deer hunting on the mountain, or the grouse shooting. The grouse shooting was marvelous, because every now and then when things got dry a steam engine hauling freight would reach a curve on the grade, throttle down, and throw off showers of sparks, and a fire would start in the fallen leaves and would streak up the mountain. In the summer, in the burned-over areas, the huckleberries and blueberries would be as high as a man's knee, and the grouse flourished on such food, in such cover. Sometimes the hunters themselves started the fires, and even today some of them believe the sanctuary should do controlled burning on the mountain for the sake of the game.

The men would talk, too, about how Sam Turner and two friends of his, going out after groundhogs and honeybees, had found themselves literally surrounded by rattlesnakes—or at least, Sam's two friends had; Sam somehow avoided it, but he was nearby. Anyway, they had to kill the snakes in order to get out. The men discussed whether you could really tell the sex of a rattlesnake by its color. There were yellow ones and black ones, and some said the yellow ones were the females, but when those three had got their snakes back to Turner's that day and cut them open, both kinds were carrying eggs. What could you make of that?

The Turners had run their hotel for sixteen years, and Sam's brother had sold out to a man from Allentown, but the old name, Schaumboch's, clung to the place like grapevine. Old Schaumboch, keeping the inn in the middle of the last century, was said to have murdered many of his guests for what they carried—they were traveling peddlers, mostly—and there were dozens of stories about that, and about the ghosts that haunted Schaumboch's. According to Sam Turner, on the night that old Mrs. Schaumboch died —her husband had been dead for many years—the doors of the hotel opened and slammed, opened and slammed, and the bottles shook on the shelves. That was what Sam Turner said, but he had a reputation as a story fabricator. Whatever you might think of *that* one, knowing Sam Turner, even so, the tales of ghosts at Schaumboch's persisted.

When the gathering at the store took place on a Saturday night in the fall, and the weather was turning cold, promising a north wind for the next day, there might well be talk of going hawk shooting. Hunting was illegal in Pennsylvania on a Sunday—except when you were hunting "vermin"—and hawks were treated as vermin not only in practice but in law. So in the morning, or perhaps after the noon meal, they got in their cars or hiked up the dreadful dirt road across the mountain until they reached a steep and rocky trail that led up to the quarry. The quarry was now defunct, and had been since the 1890's—the sand, it is said, had to be milled too much and it had too much iron in it, and then the sandhouse burned down. From the quarry, they climbed out onto the North Lookout, which they called the Point, to see which way the hawks were flying. If the wind was in the northwest, the birds might be coming right overhead, and the men would stay put and start shooting. There was no need for them to hide behind the boulders. The hawks, Charles Mohl says, "came right up to you. Sometimes you thought they'd crawl in your barl." If the wind had backed around toward the east or south overnight, the hawks might be leaving the ridge before they reached the Point and flying across the Kettle toward the other outcroppings, and then the gunners worked their way down there, sometimes all the way to the road. On a good, strong north wind, especially in October, the sharpshins might be streaming along the north face of the mountain, hugging the treetops, and the Slide would be the place to stand. The quarrymen had

(49)

cleared the Slide for some distance on either side of the tracks, to protect them from falling trees, and the scrub oak and rhododendron and laurel had not yet grown up very far. You'd go down there "a piece way," and pick off the hawks as they cleared the trees in front of you.

It was great fun. "It was nothing to go up there with two or three boxes of shells and get rid of them. The hawks usually came in flocks. Fellow lived over here used to say they leave them out in bagsful, and when a flock came he says, 'Here come another bagful.' "

The Drehersville shooters tried to keep the place pretty much to themselves. They didn't do much talking about it, certainly not out of town. But the secrecy didn't last. As Charles Mohl remembers it, one Sunday afternoon, a gang was collecting to go up the mountain, and a man from Schuylkillhaven, who knew the whole crowd, saw them standing around with their guns.

"He says, 'Where you going, boys?' We told him hawk shooting. 'Yes,' he says, 'hawk shooting.' Someone says, 'Does you want some?' 'Yes, I'll take all you get.' He didn't think we'd shoot but one, and he could have it mounted. 'All right.' And that was all that was said, and we went up, and it just happened to be a good day, and we brought these hawks along down. We got a box—a wooden box; that time, everything came in barls or wooden boxes—and this box was, I'd say, between three and four feet long, two feet high, and about two feet wide, as close as I can remember. And we threw these hawks in there, and it was all but full. We sent it to him, and that was where the blunder came in. He had a shoe factory out there, and we sent it collect, by express. And the man from the express company brought it in, and who was there but a shoe manufacturer from Pottsville. He seen this, and he was a hunter, and the next thing you knew, we had more company up there than you can place a stick at. *Everybody* was there. The game warden wanted to go up. He wasn't no shooter; he couldn't shoot. He gave his shells to everybody and his gun to anybody that didn't have none. He says, 'Shoot, and here are the shells.' And we shot a bunch of hawks, and so he got them together and hung them on a string in a ring, and he stood in the middle of them. And they took a picture of him. There was a bunch—I'd say was 25, 30, maybe 50 hawks, and they had those pictures in the Philadelphia *Record* and they had them in I don't know what-all papers. That brought more in, and more. It was nice up there, and people just came from all over and everywhere—and spoiled the whole works."

The operation became big-time, with shooting on the weekdays as well as on the weekends. Some of the hunters—including the shoeman from Pottsville and his various brothers and cousins—would carry up whole cases of shells and store them out of the weather under rocks, so that they didn't have to tote up ammunition every trip. A local sporting-goods store took a truck up there on weekends, parked on the road, and opened for business. The shoemen brought along extra guns, loaded them, and as the day's shooting began, they would tell their companions, "Ah, if they come fast, boys, don't be afraid to pick up one of these and keep firing." The shooting could be so good that the guns overheated, and if you didn't accept the shoemen's invitation, or bring along an extra gun or two of your own, you might use a specially made handle for the barrel of your gun, to protect your forward hand from the heat of the barrel—that is, said lean, old Charles Mohl drily, rapping his cane on the arms of his metal lawn chair, if you didn't respect your gun. "Some people don't care for their guns. They just keep on firing. If you have any respect for your gun, you leave some hawks go through, sometimes."

"It wasn't even safe no more to go up," he said. "When this thing was advertised, it wasn't nothing to be 50 hunters up there." Some days there were 300 or 400 shooters blazing away at one time. At least one man I know—Charles Thomas, who now runs an antique store in nearby Hamburg—and surely more men than he, could personally account for more than 100 hawks some days. Charley Thomas, slowed by a stroke a few years ago, tells hoarsely, deliberately, of one day when they counted 300 and some dead hawks all told, and he calls that outstanding; but it seems likely that the combination of thousands of passing hawks and hundreds of shooters must at times have meant the killing of many more birds than that in a day. When he looked down into the scrub below the shooting stand on a good day, Charley Thomas says, the down feathers from the bellies of the shot hawks "would hang in the branches, and I swear to Christ, it looked like a cotton tree. And *stink!*—"

They came home with good stories to tell. Most of the gunning was done with shotguns, which have an effective range of only 60 or 70 yards, if the hunter is using commercial ammunition. As Charles Mohl put it, "Hawk shooting was gauging, to know how close they are before you pull trigger." At one point, to be sure, people began bringing .22 rifles—fine sport, trying to pick off a flying bird with a rifle—but the game warden tried to put a stop to that, because it presented a considerable danger to the gunners on the mountain and the citizenry down below. One day, Charley Thomas and a friend went up the mountain, and they took along the friend's grandfather. "His grandpop shot muzzleloader. He was a blacksmith, he made his own little pistols and everything else. He had a long rifle, but bored out; he used it for shot. A broadwing come over, it was too high to shoot, and he happened to look up at us, he was down below us, and we pointed up, and he looks up, and he points this blunderbuss—*ka-BOOM!* and a big puff of smoke, and we could hear the shot smack the wings. You know what I mean. Down it comes. Tollie says, 'Grandpop, what the hell are you shootin'?' 'Why,' he says, 'bicycle ball bearings.' I says, 'No wonder he hit the hawk. Those things would go across the valley.'"

But the heyday was about over. The story of the gunning above Drehersville had spread beyond the hunting fraternity. George Miksch Sutton, an ornithologist and bird artist, was the state ornithologist and a staff-member of the State Board of Game Commissioners. In the June 1928 issue of the prestigious ornithological journal the *Wilson Bulletin* he offered some "Notes on a Collection of Hawks from Schuylkill County, Pennsylvania." A game warden had reported to the commission, Sutton wrote, about "a remarkable migration of hawks . . . occurring at certain points along Blue Mountain." Hoping to learn more about it and perhaps to gather some specimens, Sutton had gone up to Drehersville the previous October and apparently visited the Sand-head for a couple of days. The hawking wasn't too good, but two days after Sutton left, the game warden was able to report that he and a number of other shooters had just "secured, in a remarkably short time, a total of ninety Sharp-shins, sixteen Goshawks, eleven Cooper's Hawks, . . . thirty-two Red-tailed Hawks, . . . and two Duck Hawks. . . ." Those made up the bulk of the collection that Sutton described in his paper.

Now a professor emeritus in zoology at the University of Oklahoma, Sutton remembers hearing from ornithologists who were glad he had found some scientific use to which the dead hawks could be put. But what the response of the general public was, he does not know, and neither do I. It is known that T. Gilbert Pearson, then president of the National Association of Audubon Societies, told an American Game Conference in New York the winter of 1929 that his office had received "many complaints of gunners shooting hawks in their line of flight during the period of the fall migration." There had been a lot of it going on, not only in the Appalachians, but along the coast, at such places as Cape May, New Jersey, and Fisher's Island, in Long Island Sound. Some years, the autumnal Fisher's Island bag had totaled 14,000 birds of prey, or more.

In the fall of 1931, the American Society for the Prevention of Cruelty to Animals got wind of what was going on at Drehersville and complained with considerable energy to the state police. The A.S.P.C.A. must have heard that the gunners were using wounded hawks and crows as decoys—poking them with sticks to make them scream and so bring the passing hawks closer—and that a lot of the hawks that were shot down were not killed but only wounded, and were left to die slow and painful deaths where they fell. The police sent two troopers up to the mountain; they stayed three weeks, had little success, and gave the whole thing up as hopeless.

That same year, George Sutton, who was by now at Cornell University, earning his doctorate, and about to become the university's curator of birds, published another paper in the *Wilson Bulletin*, this one on the status of the goshawk in Pennsylvania. In 1929, the commonwealth had placed a \$5 bounty on goshawks; the following year, some 76 of these big, fast Accipiters had been turned in at Harrisburg—along with 427 other dead hawks which the gunners evidently *thought* were goshawks. Sutton remarked on the concentration of records of goshawks shot at Drehersville, particularly in the two years before the bounty was offered, and reviewed briefly what he knew of the migration there.

One man who read the article was Richard Pough, a young Philadelphia photographer. Pough was a birder; he would leave photography before long and go on to a distinguished career as writer and doer in conservation. At the time, he was interested by the idea that migrating hawks used the ridges; not much was known about the hawk migration in those days, and he thought he'd take a trip out to Drehersville the next fall and explore a bit. "So in the middle of September 1932, feeling sort of silly, I just went off by myself, not taking anybody with me, though I usually went birding with others. I got poking up there, and finally hit paydirt." A local farmer pointed him up the road toward Eckville and told him where to stop his car. When Pough got there, "It sounded like a battle was going on off in the distance. I followed the path toward the sound, until I got up on the lookout, and there were about a hundred Pennsylvania Dutchmen up there, all with shotguns, and having a hell of a good time. They were kidding each other in Pennsylvania Dutch—I couldn't understand a word they were saying—and they were blazing away at these birds that came by. It didn't look as if they were getting more than one out of every ten, because some trigger-happy nut would shoot when they were still out of range, and the bird would veer, and go on off. I almost figured all these young hawks were getting a good college education on the way south, as to how far a shotgun would carry." But his reaction at the moment was not so lighthearted. He saw 60 birds shot, and in a small patch of ground downhill from the Point, he found over 100 dead hawks and a great many wounded birds. He came back the next weekend with his brother, who was his partner in the photography business, and two friends. They wanted to get a better idea of how many hawks were being killed, and to photograph the evidence. They arrived on what Charley Thomas later described as "not a killing day." The hawking was poor. But two of the young men climbed down off the lookout into the brush below and began picking up hawks—230 of them in one small area. "They went down into the scrub oaks," snorted Charley Thomas, "and laced them up, stinky ones and everything, and laid them out. It sort of stressed—you know what I mean, psychological warfare."

"There were," wrote Dick Pough's friend Henry H. Collins, Jr., "without doubt, many more lying about which insufficient time alone prevented us from gathering, and this collection was made under a part of only one of the shooting stands. Most of the specimens were quite fresh, none more than three weeks old, and most less than a week."

They photographed the ranks of dead hawks, and those photographs were to become some of the most famous weapons in the conservation movement's subsequent fight to stop the hawk shooting.

The conservation movement was by no means unified in its attitude toward birds of prey. To begin with, it had as a background centuries of man-centered opinions of hawks, epitomized by ornithologist William Brewster's entry in his Concord, Massachusetts, journal for July 28, 1892. Brewster had seen a falcon that he thought was a merlin, or pigeon hawk—a dark bird about 10 inches long, with a wingspan of about two feet; it had flown in amongst a swirling flock of purple martins, which are members of the swallow family. "For a moment or two," wrote Brewster, "it sailed about with [the martins] as if it meant them no harm but merely wished to join the flock.

"None of the Martins tried, so far as I could see," Brewster continued, "to avoid it but all continued their slow, easy circling flight. Perhaps they were too frightened or bewildered . . . or more probably the majority were young, unaware of the fearful risk they were running. . . . The [hawk], secure of his prey, doubtless found a certain savage pleasure in prolonging the moment of his triumph as a Cat plays with her mouse or bird. . . .

"But at length there was a sudden dash, the flock were scattered in every direction, and a single Martin closely pursued by the Hawk disappeared behind a cluster of trees. The next instant I heard the screams of the poor victim, at first loud, then fainter, and finally, after a moment of silence, coming again in feeble despairing tones as the unfortunate creature drew its last breaths in the grasp of the sharp and relentless talons.

"As on several former occasions . . . I was moved by deep pity and fierce wrath to an extent surprising on the part of one who . . . has killed thousands of birds without suffering more than an occasional slight qualm. [Field ornithology until this century lacked good optical equipment, and when a man went birding he often took his gun along, to kill the birds he wanted to identify or study.] But there is something peculiarly moving and piteous in the voice of a bird in the clutches of a Hawk, a quality of mingled pain and apprehension which the grasp of the human hand seldom or never elicits."

This pompous attitude was carried over into "enlightened" conservation. The members of state game commissions were chiefly interested in the relationship of birds of prey to small game that hunters liked to find plentiful when they went gunning in the fall; the agricultural conservationists looked at hawks from the viewpoint of agricultural economics. Each bird of prey ate certain kinds of foods that might or might not be considered harmful to man's best interests, and those best interests varied, depending on who was making the judgment. A certain kind of hawk might take few chickens but would take a great many ducks, for example.

And any bird lover who took the trouble to study the lists of hawks' stomach contents—a feature included in a number of bird books of the day—could draw his own conclusions about the good and the bad, depending on whether or not he objected to anything in a hawk's diet. He could see that even the least harmful and most economically beneficial of the hawks sometimes transgressed and ate other birds; and there were a few hawks that ate an awful lot of mice, but also ate an awful lot of songbirds. On the whole, a great many birders distrusted hawks and thought that only a few, or perhaps none of them, should be protected.

Another difficulty with the beneficial-or-harmful approach was that once it "proved" the harmfulness of certain species, this might well be translated into laws that protected some hawks and not others. The license to shoot unprotected hawks was really a license to shoot all kinds of hawks. As I said, the hunters, generally, didn't know one hawk from another, and they didn't much care; if they were caught shooting a protected species, they could always claim ignorance, and game wardens were generally more sympathetic to the hunter than to the hawk. The state of New Jersey protected all but four species of birds of prey by the late 20's, but hunters paid no attention to what was protected and what was not, and the National Association of Audubon Societies finally felt obliged to post a trained ornithologist to the famous hawk-shooting grounds at Cape May in the fall to help the game warden educate the gunners and keep them honest.

But the greatest deficiency in the beneficial or harmful approach was that it simply ignored all the rules of nature. The case of the Accipiters was particularly interesting. These, of all the birds of prey, were the most generally disliked. They eat a great many other birds, including poultry, game birds, and songbirds.

Forest dwellers, they are short-winged and long-tailed —a configuration that gives them speed and maneuverability between the trees. All three species fly in a manner that makes them easily identifiable as Accipiters, at least in the open—a few flaps and a glide, a few flaps and a glide. The adults of all three are gray-backed—almost blue-gray, which gives them the common name, blue darters.

The goshawk, biggest of the three, hunter of pheasant and grouse and squirrels and rabbits, is finely marked with gray on the breast and belly, where its smaller cousins are cinnamon-colored; and it has a bright white line over the eye that circles its head like a crown. Its round-tipped wings stretch 40 to 47 inches across, and from beak to the end of its tail, it measures 20 to more than 26 inches. As with most birds of prey, the female is bigger and heavier than the male. The gos is a bird of much courage, often attacking fiercely anyone who approaches the vicinity of its nest, never mind tries to climb the nest tree, and stories are legion about goshawks that were shot at while raiding chicken yards and came right back for another pass. "One day in the great British Columbian forest," wrote Edward Howe Forbush, a leading ornithologist in the first three decades of this century, "I had a good opportunity to collect a number of Long-crested Jays as a flock passed me high overhead among the tall trees. I had shot three or four when I noticed that not one had reached the ground. Shooting another I watched it fall, when a Western Goshawk swept out from among the trees into the very smoke from my gun and snatched it in the air."

It is known to hurl itself into a bush after prey that has gone to cover there, if not to grapple the prey, at least to drive it out into the open again. One observer followed goshawk tracks in the snow; these goshawks seemed to be on the trails of rabbits—on foot all the way—and at the end of some of these trails, the ornithologist found dead rabbits, partially eaten. A hawk on foot, *tracking?* And Audubon saw a goshawk flying after a large flock of blackbirds as it crossed over a river. "The Hawk approached them with the swiftness of an arrow, when the Blackbirds rushed together so closely that the flock looked like a dusky ball passing through the air. On reaching the mass, he, with the greatest ease, seized first one, then another, and another, giving each a squeeze with his talons, and suffering it to drop upon the water. In this manner, he had procured four or five before the poor birds reached the woods, into which they instantly plunged, when he gave up the chase, swept over the water in graceful curves, and picked up the fruits of his industry, carrying each bird singly to the shore. Reader, is this instinct or reason?"

That was a hunt in the open, and the prey was not taken by surprise. Often, a gos will streak along the edge of a wood—almost invisible just below the treetops (I've seen one do that, going at least 40 miles an hour on the level, cruising speed), or will sit quietly on a perch, waiting for something to move, and then sail swiftly down on its prey before the victim has a chance to move.

The smaller cousins—the medium-sized Cooper's hawk and the little sharpshin—operate on the same model, but usually hunt smaller prey. All were admired for their flair and bravery—and hated. The goshawk, to Neltje Blanchan, a popular nature writer at the turn of the century, was "a villain of deepest dye. Grouse, Bob Whites, ducks, and rabbits:—in fact, all the sportsman's pets [*pets!*] and innumerable songbirds, are hunted down with a dash and spirit worthy of a better motive."

Somehow, the goshawk and the grouse, the Cooper's and the sharpshin and the songbirds, had managed to coexist for many thousands of years, without the prey species vanishing. There was evidence enough of that. Certainly, only recently have we learned much about the mechanics of predator-prey relationships, thanks in large part to a pioneering study by two brothers, John J. and Frank C. Craighead, Jr. It has now been demonstrated that under natural circumstances birds of prey feed on the surplus of prey populations—that is, the birds and animals that have bred to numbers that cannot be sustained by the best cover and food available and so must make themselves vulnerable in order to survive; such vulnerability increases the chances of their being preyed upon. Predation also tends to weed out the unhealthy and weaker members of prey populations and to eliminate from a breeding population the "sports" that are conspicuously colored or otherwise built in a way that makes them more vulnerable than their fellows. Except when the prey population is in serious trouble from other causes—such as over-hunting—birds of prey only check population growth and can do no serious damage to it. They cannot prevent plagues of mice or rabbits, for example, without help from other limiting factors, such as fluctuating food availability, bad weather, disease, and other predators. And once a plague gets started, hawks and owls can do no more than skim off the top of the mouse or rabbit population.

So hawks were neither as important by themselves to the control of crop pests as the agriculturalists of the 30's believed, nor as important in the destruction of game as the hunters thought—unless they had the help of hunters or a famine or some other disaster to the prey. But certain naturalists had an inkling of the facts. "In Nova Scotia and New Brunswick," wrote John Birchard May in his book *The Hawks of North America* in 1935, "where the Goshawk is a summer resident, the Ruffed Grouse flourishes wherever it is not overshot, despite the presence of this predator."

So American conservationists included among their number not only birders who thought all hawks were bad and some who thought only some hawks were bad, but also a few who believed that badness or goodness in the eyes of man should not decide the question of protection; certainly if a hawk were caught taking a farmer's pullets, they said, the farmer had a right to dispatch that one hawk (if he couldn't bring himself to cage over his hens so the hawk had no way to get at them), but he shouldn't be allowed to go after the whole tribe of hawks. As one writer put it, "If one should see a man in a blue suit making his escape after having robbed a house, and should thereupon sally forth into the street with a shotgun and blaze away at every man in a blue suit that he happened to meet, he would be carrying out in practice the principle upon which many act when they wage indiscriminate warfare upon our native hawks."

Richard Pough and friends made five trips, all told, that fall of 1932, to observe the "indiscriminate warfare" being waged from the top of Blue Mountain at Drehersville. The November–December issue of *Bird-Lore*—published for the National Association of Audubon Societies—printed a letter from Pough about the "appalling slaughter" in Pennsylvania, which Pough believed was much worse than it had ever been at Cape May—which was saying a good deal.

For his part, Pough's friend Henry Collins wrote a long and detailed description of their Drehersville experiences for the annual report of the Hawk and Owl Society, which had just been organized that spring in New Jersey.

Protests were lodged with the Pennsylvania Game Commission, with no results. Collins and Pough even complained to the Lord's Day Alliance about the Sunday shooting of hawks. Their goal at the time was to get the hawk shooting outlawed one way or the other, but by the following fall nothing had changed.

However, the conservation community around New York City—including the national office of Audubon, the prestigious Linnaean Society of New York, the Hawk and Owl Society, and the Emergency Conservation Committee—was now becoming aware of the situation in Drehersville, and Pough and Collins were asked to come up from Philadelphia that October to address a special meeting. In the audience for the meeting were a number of leading lights in the conservation movement, including the chairman of the Emergency Conservation Committee, Mrs. Rosalie Barrow Edge. A former suffragette then in her mid-fifties, a woman of strong opinions and often overbearing manner, Rosalie Edge was once described by an admirer as "the only honest, unselfish, indomitable hellcat in the history of conservation." She looked rather like Eleanor Roosevelt, and sounded a great deal like her, too. Mrs. Edge's committee had been started partly in response to what she and others thought was (to put it kindly) the stodginess of conservation organizations, particularly the Audubon Societies. Conservation, they felt, needed aggressive, militant activists to carry the fight to save vanishing wildlife and wilderness, and at the time it seemed to them that the major organizations, trying to keep their diverse constituencies happy, were playing things rather close to the vest. So the committee took up the cudgels. It had conducted strident campaigns to protect waterfowl, the bald eagle, elk, antelope, sugar pines in Yosemite National Park, and the integrity of the national parks. As it happened, the committee's running battle with the national organizations was to get hotter because of what happened at and after this special meeting. Twenty-seven years later, it still rankled in Rosalie Edge's memory. The sense of the meeting was that the promontory above Drehersville should be made a sanctuary—the world's first sanctuary for birds of prey; hawk shooting was unlikely to be outlawed quickly in Pennsylvania. "A society of wide renown and great wealth [this was Audubon, although Mrs. Edge would not deign to name the society] . . . promised (so we conservationists believed) to purchase the property and give sanctuary to the persecuted birds. We experienced a lively sense of relief. We rejoiced the more because we believed that the new sanctuary would be born with a silver spoon in its mouth, and that a ring of fairy godmothers would stand around its cradle." But National Audubon took no action during the next year.

Procrastination was more dangerous to the hawks than any of the conservationists knew. Hawk Mountain had been up for sale, cheap, for years. "It lay for taxes for quite a while," remembered Charles Mohl, sitting in his lawn chair with the mountain at his back. "We had a little gun club around here, and we wanted to buy it." There was some question, however, about whether the gun club really needed all that land. "And we didn't have that much money in the treasury, but I guess we could have got it together. We just left it go and left it go . . ."

In the summer of 1934, Mrs. Edge got in touch with Dick Pough and asked what had happened about Hawk Mountain. "So far as I know, nothing," he told her. Audubon's inaction was to her like a bugle sounding the charge, and she decided that this was a job for the Emergency Conservation Committee. She and Pough went out to Drehersville to explore the situation, and shortly thereafter she arranged to lease the 1,398 acres for a year, for $500, with an option to buy for $3000 more. The $500 down came from another member of the E.C.C., Dr. Willard G. Van Name, who was a curator at the American Museum of Natural History and a vigorous champion of hawks.

Now that the property was at least temporarily in the hands of conservationists, a potential sanctuary, someone had to be hired to make it a sanctuary in fact by being on hand during the gunning season and keeping out the hunters. Mrs. Edge had someone in mind for the job. There was a young ornithologist, mostly self-taught, a slender, bright, dogged fellow who had already managed two private wildlife refuges very successfully. His name was Maurice Broun. He and his bride, Irma, had just moved to Vermont, where Maurice was taking over another refuge.

He was already something of a Horatio Alger figure in ornithology. In later life, he didn't much like to talk about his beginnings, but his wife would a little: "I'll have you know that this man raised himself. His mother died when he was two weeks old. His father died when he was two years old. They were people from Roumania, and they came over here, and they died of TB. He was put in a New York City orphanage, where he didn't see grass or a tree until he was taken out by a Catholic family—he was younger than seven, then. The mother became ill, and the foster father brought Maurice back to the terrible orphanage; the man who ran it was sadistic and used to beat the kids up once every week—Saturday night, they were automatically beaten with a strap. When he was ten, a Jewish family came in and took him to Boston. He ran away from his foster home when he was fifteen, and he has earned his own bread and butter since that time." Neither of the Brouns would talk about why he ran away, but it may well be that birds had something to do with it.

One spring day, in his fourteenth year, he was on his way across Boston Public Garden when he came upon a group of adults standing around under a freshly leafed tree and staring up into it through binoculars. He stopped and tried to make out what they were looking at. One of the grownups noticed him and offered him her binoculars. With the aid of the glasses he found a magnolia warbler and was instantly bird-struck. The dramatically marked warbler, bright yellows and blacks and whites and grays, was, he later wrote, "truly the most . . . beautiful thing my eyes had ever beheld."

And so Maurice Broun became a birdwatcher—before long, a very good one. Dick Pough first met him "when Maurice was a high school student and I was at M.I.T., and he used to lead bird walks in the Boston Public Garden. I remember his going with the Brookline Bird Club on a trip to Ipswich [on the shore north of Boston] on, I think it was, New Year's Day. A bitter cold day, and Broun came along with, actually, his bare toes showing out of his shoes. We were all worried about him freezing his feet, because we walked all the way from the station out to the marsh, which was four or five miles. And the story was that his father was a Russian Jewish tailor, and they just thought this boy of theirs was *nuts*, and they did everything they could to discourage him, but nothing would. He even printed a little booklet I think I still have somewhere, on the birds of the Boston Public Garden."

In any case, Maurice left home. He supported himself through public school by working as a bus boy and working in a hospital laundry. After he graduated, he bellhopped at the Women's City Club of Boston. In his free time, he birded wherever his meager finances permitted him to go around Boston. Usually, he went only so far as he could travel by trolley and shank's mare. He remembers many a time he went out collecting discarded milk bottles to cash in for the necessary carfare, but when he could get someplace on foot, he did, and he had the long, quick stride that seems to have been characteristic of New England birders of that era—about twice as fast and twice as long as a normal step.

He made a good friend of the lady who had offered her

binoculars and so brought him into the world of birds, Edith McLellan Hale. She was obviously very impressed with him, and when Maurice was twenty, she talked about him to her friend Edward Howe Forbush. Dr. Forbush was the pre-eminent ornithologist in a state that boasted dozens of leading bird men. With the help of John Birchard May, he was then working on the third and last volume of his monumental *Birds of Massachusetts and Other New England States*, which was being published by the Commonwealth of Massachusetts. Mrs. Hale talked Forbush into hiring Maurice Broun, and for the next three years Maurice received what amounted to a graduate-school education in ornithology.

In the Forbush work, each species was discussed at length in a narrative that drew on the experiences of Forbush and many other birders; these "Haunts and Habits," as the sections were called, are still considered classics of the genre. Each Haunts and Habits was preceded by about two pages of fine print, which described in technical detail the physical characteristics of the male of the species, the female, and the young birds, the various molts, the field marks that helped a birder identify them in the field, the voice, the breeding habits, the range, and the distribution in New England. Putting this material together involved a great deal of digging in old texts and ornithological journals, and it was to that job that Forbush assigned Maurice Broun. After a while, Forbush also asked him to write a few of the Haunts and Habits—among them, the yellow-throat, the black-capped chickadee, the hermit thrush, and two little-known hybrids, the Brewster's and Lawrence's warblers—and he acquitted himself well. "But did I read," Maurice said, remembering the writing-up of the hybrids. "I never rested a second. I worked day and night, because I had to do my regular work, and then I'd go to my little cubbyhole of a room—in a place called Claremont street in Boston—and I'd have all these books with me, and reports, and so on under my arm, and I'd have to wade through them, pick out the meat, and make notes, and then when I thought I had all the data I needed, then I sat right down and wrote. I never took a minute. I can still see myself as a young man, slaving away. I didn't take time to eat anything—I ate *candy*."

In the fall of 1929 (Maurice was now twenty-three years old), Forbush and May learned of a job opening in Lenox, in western Massachusetts, where the local bird club was setting up the Pleasant Valley Bird Sanctuary. Maurice could have stayed on until the book was done, but they believed he should take the job, and they set about convincing him and the people in Lenox that he was the man for the position. The Lenox people, said Maurice, *had* to be convinced. "They were very dubious. I had no background, I was young." But the recommendation of these two deans of Massachusetts birding was very compelling, and late in the fall, he went out to Lenox for $1,800 a year. For the next three years he carved out the new sanctuary—six miles of nature trails and a museum.

"From time to time, I would get a brochure or a circular from the Emergency Conservation Committee. Here was this woman in New York City who was *doing* things in conservation—very militant, very strident, very abrasive, but she was *doing* things. Getting things done. With every piece of literature she sent out, there was an appeal, and I sent her 10 bucks. Which for me was a hell of a lot of money. In fact, I was crazy. She always acknowledged the money, and so one day I wrote her and said, 'You don't have to acknowledge this. Glad to do it.' "

That letter led Rosalie Edge to invite him to visit her in New York, and later, in 1932, after he had changed jobs and was running the Austin Research Station on Cape Cod, to invite herself and a friend for a March weekend at the station—a visit that turned into a series of wide-ranging birding trips led by Maurice.

By 1934 Maurice was ready to move on again. This time he took with him a pretty and slight Cape Codder, an artist, as his wife, and Irma's influence would before long begin to temper his tendency to overdo things, to drive himself at his work until he was exhausted and sick of it.

"I didn't know how to relax. I'd work 20 hours a day, and I'd do this endlessly." They went to Vermont, to the Green Mountains, where Maurice had agreed to develop another private wildlife sanctuary. They were scarcely settled in, however, when a letter arrived from Rosalie Edge. The Emergency Conservation Committee had leased Hawk Mountain in Pennsylvania, and it needed someone to take charge of the place during the fall. Were the Brouns available, and for how much? "I'd read all about this place in *Bird-Lore*," Maurice recalled, "and I knew what the situation was and what she was up against." In a day or two, he wrote back that yes, they were available for the fall, and they'd do it for room and board and expenses.

THREE

On the north edge of North Lookout, near the top, with the slope of the mountain dropping precipitously to the valley more or less under his left elbow, the lean and boyish Frank Haas has staked out his regular seat—one boulder to sit on, another to lean against. He has folded his pale-blue quilted jacket for a cushion, stashed his backpack beside him where he can get into it for the Coke and sandwiches and chocolate bars with which he sustains himself, and now settles into his niche to wait for the lifting of the fog, which washes the flanks of the ridge below him like a sea through which the peaks of the ridge jut, like islands.

Frank manages four small state parks, northwest of Hawk Mountain, but almost all his days off between the first of August and the tenth of December are spent here. This setting up for the day on the lookout is a ritual he has gone through many hundreds of times by now. He was raised over in Minersville, not far from the mountain, began coming here in his middle teens, and waited out the month before he went into the Army by spending every fair day on the lookouts. During the month, he became very good at identifying hawks and left home so hooked on hawks that in Vietnam he got the rest of the men in his headquarters outfit trained to shout whenever they saw birds of prey overhead, which usually brought him racing out of his office with his binoculars. When his tour was up, he returned to the mountain; that entire fall he stayed with his parents in Minersville and came up here every day the hawks were flying, and a good many when they were not, which gave the sanctuary a full-time extra man, a volunteer, to take the count or, in poor weather, do some other job.

Frank is just one example among many Hawk Mountain regulars who follow that tradition. There have always been more jobs to do here than people to do them, and a number of birders who came at first just to watch hawks have pitched in to fill the gaps.

The Brouns themselves set the pattern that first fall of 1934, offering to come down from New England at no pay. The Emergency Conservation Committee insisted on giving Maurice a salary, but Irma remained a volunteer. Many years later, when she was still a full-time assistant to her husband, she was on the books at $200 a year; being a sparky lady, tough enough to stand up to loaded hunters carrying loaded shotguns, she remonstrated with Mrs. Edge, who—being a sparky lady herself—replied that Irma ought to consider herself as a minister's wife and be glad to work for nothing. In a way, that was outrageous, yet the sense of mission was part of the sanctuary from the beginning, and the Brouns encouraged it.

People—particularly young people—arrived at Hawk Mountain and were immediately attracted to the energetic and devoted Brouns. Above all, Maurice was "a tremendous field naturalist," in the words of Roland Clement, now National Audubon's vice president for biology. Clement's first job in conservation was working for Maurice at the Austin Research Station on the Cape. "He is a wonderful naturalist, a wonderful ornithologist, a wonderful botanist," says Clement, "although his lack of formal education for years kept him from the full recognition he deserved." Maurice assumed that any hawkwatcher would be as excited about the sanctuary as he was, and his enthusiasm was catching. He was also a natural teacher. Tom Hanson, one of his early Hawk Mountain protégés, who recently quit a successful career in business to teach science, remembers what his exposure to Maurice meant: "Here was a person who had probably more innate knowledge concerning ornithology and botany and the other natural sciences than any other 10 or 12 people. And at that age—in my teens—I just soaked it up, just like a sponge."

The Brouns invited visitors in for a cup of coffee or tea and a piece of pie; put them up on rainy weekends; gathered them around for impromptu lectures or birding talk; and in general treated them as partners in the enterprise. A family was forming, and the members of that family would find themselves, on rainy or foggy days when the hawks weren't in the air, helping Maurice string wire around the boundaries—miles of wire—or burning brush or chopping firewood or building camping shelters. Maurice could sometimes scrape together enough money to hire one of the youngsters (as Tom Hanson, for example) at $50 a month for the summer. But there wasn't much money available. Hawk Mountain Sanctuary ran then, as it does now, on membership dues, gifts, a small admissions fee, and profits from the sales of books and the like; and in those days, with only a few hundred members in the association, the annual income wasn't large. So various members of this sanctuary-cum-family set aside a week or a month or the better part of a season to come to Hawk Mountain and help the Brouns, for free. They patrolled the bounds to keep out the hunters, stood in for Maurice to take the count of hawks—it was an honor to be asked —built trails and fireplaces and outhouses; they laid down phone lines for communication on the mountain; they gave furniture and field glasses and plants and handmade signs.

Though it was hard to create and run a sanctuary on the sort of finances available to Hawk Mountain in the early years, at the same time the fact that the sanctuary hadn't been born with a silver spoon in its mouth and fairy godmothers standing around the cradle gave it a very special quality. The Brouns and Tom Hanson have remained close friends; when Maurice needs help with heavy work around the farm that he has, since he retired, turned into a personal ecological study area, Tom joins him. That gives an idea of the kinds of bonds Maurice and Irma created, and the feeling that their "family" had and has for Hawk Mountain. Maurice and Tom talked about it recently. "We actually, physically, built the place," Tom said. "In that sense, it became mine. I built it. I know all the *boards* there. I know the trails, because I cut them."

"Do you remember the time," put in Maurice excitedly, leaning forward in his chair, with an intensity that always gives one the feeling there's a spring compressed inside him, "we got together a lot of material and boards and built a latrine, all for under $25? And weren't we proud of it? First we had to dig a tremendous hole—"

"—In the rocks—"

"And then we built a *magnificent* latrine, for less than $25."

Finances are not so tight as they once were, and the old-timers—having been pioneers—may feel a bit superior toward most of the present membership. But there are a good many newer members of the sanctuary association, living within a day's travel of the sanctuary, who donate a lot of time and energy to various tasks at Hawk Mountain. The sense of family remains, years after the Brouns left. It is one of their most valuable legacies.

Some of the members work around the place, some lead groups of youngsters on ecology walks on the trails, some help take the count. But one of the most interesting volunteer projects is Tom Mutchler's work with injured hawks.

In the past, when birds of prey had wing bones broken by shot or by accident, the best that could be done for them was to splint the wing, tie it to the body, and hope. A bird's wing bones are mostly air—a column of bone around a honeycomb of bone, strong enough to bear the bird's weight in flight, light enough not to drag it down.

Setting such a bone exactly when it has been shattered, to get a good fit and a good mend, is very nearly impossible using the splinting method. Hawk Mountain has always functioned as a hospital for injured hawks, but it was extremely discouraging to watch the birds mend badly and then have to keep them around, the injured wings dragging and useless, until they died. It was no life for a hawk, and a good many of these patients had to be destroyed.

Tom Mutchler is a surgeon's assistant, a trained surgical nurse. He lives in Bethlehem, and he has been coming to Hawk Mountain for a number of years. He had watched the unsuccessful bone-setting process for hawks, and it occurred to him there might be a much better way. As it happened, his solution had already been hit upon by one veterinarian in the West, but at the time almost no one knew about it—certainly no one at Hawk Mountain. Why not, Tom suggested to Alex Nagy, try the same thing that is used on badly shattered human bones, a procedure known as pinning. Sterilize the area around the wound, anesthetize the hawk, clean out the broken fragments, and pass a thin rod of stainless steel down through the center of the bone. That would hold the fractured ends of the bone exactly in place, and a good mend would be much more likely.

It worked. The pins do such a good job fitting the fracture that one red-shouldered hawk, for example, having just been operated on, stood up and spread both wings as if nothing had happened to it. "This was not encouraged," Tom reported drily. The injured wing was immobilized with a stocking bandage, but for only three weeks; hawks quickly lay down a great deal of new bone around a fracture. After the stocking was taken off, the hawk was able to use the wing a little almost immediately, and it was returned to freedom—the pin removed—three months after the operation. The procedure is now standard at the sanctuary, with Tom acting as surgeon—backed up by two radiologists in Bethlehem who provide x-ray equipment when necessary, and act as consultants.

It took Rosalie Edge four years to raise the money and clear the title to Hawk Mountain. Then, in 1938, the Emergency Conservation Committee bought the property and turned it over to the newly organized Hawk Mountain Sanctuary Association, of which Mrs. Edge became president and remained so until her death in 1962.

The Brouns had been coming west from New England each fall. They had posted the property, and—with Irma standing guard at the entrance to the trail—Maurice had begun watching hawk migrations from the Point, which Mrs. Edge referred to as the Observation Rocks. With the help of a specially hired sheriff, they patrolled the road to keep the hunters out, and faced down angry gunners who approached the gate, their guns casually cradled in their arms so that the muzzles pointed at Maurice's or Irma's stomach. Maurice, walking the bounds during deer season, would hear a shotgun blast and then the whistle of a slug over his head. A red-tailed hawk was shot and its corpse hung as a warning from the girders of the old bridge across the Little Schuylkill River in Drehersville.

The Brouns reacted with their own gestures. Maurice, for example, photographed the dead hawk hanging from the bridge and used it to publicize the work of the sanctuary. "Broun was the most hated man," said the antique dealer Charley Thomas, "if ever there was a man hated. He's lucky he's living. I pushed a gun down one day that was pointed right at his head." And one is tempted to agree with Charley Thomas, that it was amazing they weren't killed or hurt, because the men they were dealing with—coal miners, local small businessmen, a few farmers—had reputations for roughness, and they deeply resented these out-of-towners who kept them from their hawk-shooting stands.

But this was a Pennsylvania Dutch region, strong in the tradition of property rights. Charley Thomas remarked that there had been good hawk shooting to the east of Hawk Mountain, at Bake Oven Knob in Lehigh County, but that people from Berks or Schuylkill counties didn't go up there to shoot, because that was Lehigh territory, and you didn't go hunting in someone else's territory any more than you went courting there. If you *did*, the consequences were likely to be unpleasant.

Sure, said Charles Mohl, there were a lot of people angry at the Brouns. "In words. In words. People around here understood, when you buy something, it's yours, and nobody else got no *business* there. Now, they went in, and they chased them and stuff like that, but to do them any harm, they knew better than that. So I don't think Maurice had any reason to be scared. They didn't talk *well* of him, that I *know*. But they wouldn't hurt him, and they had all the chance in the world."

During the first four autumns, the Brouns had boarded with a family down in Drehersville; not all the local people disapproved of them. Schaumboch's little hotel on the rocky mountain road—despite its history, its lack of electricity and telephone and plumbing, and its ghosts— would have done as a residence for the "warden" and his bride. But it was not part of the original property, and the owner, who had used it for a while to house a still, at first refused to sell, and then held out for a high price. In the summer of 1938, as the sanctuary association came into existence, a member of the board of directors paid the man's price, and at the end of August the Brouns moved in, to begin their first renovation of Schaumboch's.

It would always be something of a problem to maintain. It was an ancient building, with all the infirmities attendant on age. In particular, the foot-thick Blue Mountain stone walls did not hold mortar very well in the kind of weather they had to endure, so they were constantly in need of repair. When the Brouns walked into it after one long absence, Irma took one look and burst into tears. The inside walls were covered with mold and ice, and water had ruined everything it could reach and rot.

The years before the war were eye-openers at—and because of—Hawk Mountain. To begin with, there were the numbers of hawks that passed. The first year's figures weren't very useful, scientifically, because Maurice didn't start counting that year until October and often he had to interrupt his hawking to keep the posters up and the hunters off. But even at that, he had counted close to 11,000 hawks. In 1935, the totals were over 15,700; in 1936, 1,000 higher than that.

Joseph A. Hagar, an ornithologist with the Massachusetts Division of Fisheries and Game, commented in the *Massachusetts Audubon Bulletin* in 1937: "If I were to name the discovery that has stirred the widest interest among bird-lovers of the East during the last decade, it would be 'Hawk Mountain.' Ornithologists may have known for years of the great flights of hawks which drift southward in the fall through New England and the Middle Atlantic States, but recent accounts from Pennsylvania have focused general public attention on the movement as never before, and for the first time given a true understanding of its extent and regularity."

Dick Pough wrote about a group of his friends whom he led up to Hawk Mountain the first year: "I suspect that they have accepted my invitation with the belief that this would put a stop to my ridiculous stories of Golden Eagles and White Gyrfalcons in Pennsylvania. They are all active bird students and yet they all say they have not seen twenty-five Hawks of any kind in the past year." The same could be said of most active birders; they might happen to notice a soaring redtail or broadwing now and then, and see a red-shoulder pair prospecting for a nest near a swampy wood in early spring; during a walk in an upland forest, they might put up a sharpshin from her nest; or find, perched on a telephone wire above a meadow's edge, a kestrel—a small falcon, often called sparrow hawk, with a boldly marked face and lovely coloring, the male brown-backed and gray-winged, the female all brown from above; it flicks its tail as it sits, and looks down into the meadow after field mice, then casts off the perch in a gentle, stiff-winged glide, hovers, glides, hovers again, and at last pounces on its mouse; a marsh hawk might appear on the far side of that meadow, sailing along low with its wings tilted up and its badge—a white rump patch— showing when the bird wheeled; and if the birder lived near water, he might be fortunate enough to be in the vicinity of an osprey nest, or even an osprey colony. But as a rule, hawks are thinly distributed. They spend a great part of the day perched motionless and silent. The same characteristics of stealth and speed that aid the hawks in hunting make spotting them often just a matter of luck, even when they are in the air. A birder could pass an entire day in the field without noticing a one.

So the reports of *thousands* of hawks flying by a single point during the fall migration, regularly, year after year, not only came as a distinct surprise but also began drawing the more dedicated birders toward Drehersville and—though their cars might well boil over—up the washboard road toward the sanctuary. You could see more hawks there in 10 minutes of a good day than you saw the rest of the year away from the Observation Rocks; not only that, you might well see species of hawks that you would only find, with luck, once every five or ten years, otherwise. For that matter, you might *never* see some of the birds otherwise. Maurice had reported a few of the big gyrfalcons—birds that breed in the Arctic and very rarely come far south in the fall and winter. And most remarkable of all was the regular occurrence of golden eagles at Hawk Mountain: 39 had been counted flying past in the first year and 26 in the second. Man's presence had driven these big brown birds with the golden sheen on their hackles from their known breeding territories in New England, and the birding fraternity had been under the impression that golden eagles simply didn't appear in the Northeast any longer.

Through Maurice and a growing corps of hawkwatchers, whose interest blossomed because of the sanctuary, the birding fraternity at large became aware of the rhythms of the migration. The hawks did not all head south at once. The first few birds began to move in August—a scattering of broadwings, sharpshins, Cooper's hawks, kestrels, peregrines, ospreys, golden eagles, and "Florida" bald eagles that spent their summers in Maine and points east and then returned south to breed in the winter. The pace accelerated in mid-September, as the broadwing flight reached its peak; in terms of numbers, September was the biggest month, mostly because of the broadwings. By the end of the month or the beginning of October, the broadwings gave way to the major thrust of the sharpshin migration. A few more peregrines and some merlins would join the steady trickle of kestrels; but apparently most of the speedy falcons, all torpedo-shaped birds with pointed wings, migrated along the coast rather than down the Appalachians. The red-shouldered hawks would be most numerous about the same time as the sharpshins—in mid-October. The numbers of passing bald eagles would dwindle, to grow again in November, when a few of the northern breeding birds came by. The counts of redtails mounted as November approached, and sometime around the turn of the month there might be a great day or two when the wind blew like stink out of the north and hundreds of redtails flew past, along with golden and bald eagles and, some years, rough-legged hawks and goshawks from northern Canada. Those birds would make up most of what was left of the migration, and there might even be a few of them passing as late as the first week of December.

Another discovery was the migrating speed of the birds of prey. In the fall of 1942, the Brouns were joined on the mountain by a number of young men who had signed up with the Armed Forces and were waiting to be called. Two of them helped Maurice get started on an experiment, timing the flight speeds of the passing hawks in varying weather conditions. Of necessity, the experiment demanded a forward observer at the head of a measured course to help choose the hawk to be timed and to signal when it passed. This forward observer had to be in communication with the lookout, so the two young men strung a phone wire from the lookout up along the ridge two-thirds of a mile to the east, over difficult terrain— boulder field after boulder field. For the forward observer's watch a tall tree was chosen, and then one or another youthful volunteer would climb the tree and perch there, phone in hand, to mark the moment when the birds passed and to inform Maurice, who was quite literally at his post on the lookout; the telephone there was placed on the top of a sawed-off tree stub, sticking up through the rocks, and Maurice sat on a rock behind this miniature desk—from which hung a pair of high-powered binoculars and a movie camera.

During that fall, they managed to pick 152 hawks and 14 crows that flew a straight course to Maurice after passing the starting point. They timed a sharpshin doing 60 and an osprey going 80, but a peregrine—the fastest species in the world—dawdled by at 32 miles an hour. The average migrating speed of all the hawks was 30.

Maurice went to war himself in 1943, though from the Pacific he continued to make the annual $10 contribution to the sanctuary he always had. Irma took a job in Massachusetts for the duration. The sanctuary marked time. Gas rationing kept down the numbers of visitors and put a crimp in the deer hunting, so the association did not bother to hire a replacement. Volunteers stood in when they could.

The remarkable thing was that groups of hawkwatchers planned their wartime gas consumption around at least one trip to the sanctuary in a fall; they saved their coupons and packed into cars together for the journey. Others took the train and then hiked from Port Clinton, six miles away, or up the mountain from Drehersville (but the train would stop there only if there were ten or more passengers aboard who wanted to get off). One soldier on furlough visited the sanctuary with his invalid brother, whom he carried on his back up the steep trail, two-thirds of a mile, to the lookout.

What was there about the place that brought people on such pilgrimages? Certainly there were other attractions at Hawk Mountain beside the hawks. The Brouns' "boys" would write to Mrs. Edge from overseas: "There is one thing that I hope to find unchanged when this war is over, and that is Hawk Mountain. Even if the world is tearing itself apart, the hawks will continue to fly over the Sanctuary, and the days and nights will be just as peaceful and beautiful." "Three things with me are synonymous with Hawk Mountain," said another, "—peace and quiet, good fellowship, and Irma Broun's apple pie." The sense of rational purpose in nature, the friendship and dedication of the Brouns—these were ties to the mountain. So were the unusual geology of the place and, for some, the interesting botany and the migrations of other birds besides the hawks. But these were things that one might learn to appreciate after being there a while. What drew most people to the mountain at first—and what for many remained central to their joy in the place—was indeed the hawks.

Birds of prey are marvelous flyers. A robin or a warbler or a sparrow may be as talented on the wing, but it flits past, a small blur, darts from one bush and dives into another. Birds of prey, in general, are large by comparison, and in relation to their size, slower than the smaller birds; once spotted, they are conspicuous for their power and their command of the air. Particularly in the big, slow-moving Buteos and eagles, and in the furiously speedy peregrine, one sees the epitome of Flight. Man's jealousy of this skill must be one reason for his special attention.

But I think there's more to it than that. Such birds are among the premier hunters—another source of envy; their skill and range far outstripped those of primitive man the hunter. In the ancient view, they flew close to the heavens and thus were messengers of magic, gods themselves or companions to the gods. A falcon was Egypt's god of day, and Zeus was associated with eagles. The legendary and observed powers of eagles in particular made them obvious symbols of the powers of states and of kings.

Tradition and myth present the bird of prey as bigger than life, and often threatening. Sinbad's eagle, for example, put the entire earth in shadow. Malayans have an eagle god named Gerda, and when clouds sweep in to hide the sun, they say, "Gerda spreads her wings to dry them." In a few tales, men are carried off by predatory birds.

There are several species of eagles still extant that feed on monkeys—among them the crowned eagle of Africa, the harpy eagle of the Amazon rain forest, the monkey-eating eagle of the eastern Philippines, which stands higher than a man's waist. And when the black-and-chestnut eagles of the Andes "fly low over the forest . . . ," say Mary Louise Grossman and John Hamlet in *Birds of Prey of the World*, "monkeys scream and run for cover on the lowest branches." I wonder if man's fascination isn't based partly on echoes of terror that have followed us in our genetic baggage through our evolution.

To some extent, conscious terror of hawks and eagles has persisted to the present day, in the stories of babies snatched from dooryards by eagles. There has been a tendency in recent years to pooh-pooh these stories as only fables. But there is no reason to think that a hungry eagle, seeing a baby crawling unattended outside a wilderness cabin, might not have been tempted—particularly if its normal food supply was scarce or the bird had grown too old or sick to catch its regular prey.

A hawkwatcher recently told me of a woman who visited a lookout with her children for—evidently—only the scenery, and when he casually pointed out an approaching hawk, the lady hustled her brood back to the car, declaring she wouldn't allow them out in the open while there was a hawk around. One might be tempted to smile at that, but I for one have stood looking up at a low-soaring redtail and felt a bit uneasy. And Alex Nagy tells of a similar reaction. "About ten years ago, I used to fool around with a rabbit call. Well, we were up on North Lookout one November day, hiding behind the rocks, and a golden eagle came over. I blew on the rabbit call, and the eagle tucked its wings and stooped toward the lookout, braked when it saw us, and flew on off. But as it came in, it made this soft whistle, the air passing over it. The sound was like—well, you know, when we were kids, we used to grind a hole in the end of a yardstick and whirl it over our heads—a mesmerizing sound—well, it was like that. We were thrilled, but at the same time we were almost put back into a primitive state, like the first time you see a copperhead."

One oughtn't lay too great a stress on the mythic and genetic influences on hawkwatchers, but it seems obvious that curiosity and aesthetic pleasure are not the only motives that pull us up the mountain to witness the annual flight south of the birds of prey. As a friend of mine once said, "Can you imagine a *Dove* Mountain?"

In 1946 began what Maurice Broun remembers as the halcyon days at Hawk Mountain. The directors decided that the association had grown large enough—there were nearly 900 members—to warrant having the Brouns in residence throughout the year. So Maurice and Irma arrived in March, with "a pregnant goat, two pregnant dogs, a hundred pounds of alfalfa, fifty pounds of dog food, and everything we owned," and set Schaumboch's to rights. During the next ten years, the membership climbed to more than 2,500. The visitations by hawkwatchers and tourists had numbered about 3,000 in 1941; it was more than 4,000 that first year after the war, and ten years later, more than 11,000. Regularly there were cars from as far away as Massachusetts, Ohio, and Ontario parked along the road on fall weekends, and sometimes people came from much farther away than that; Hawk Mountain was known all over the country, all over the world. (A Connecticut neighbor remembers the first time he heard—with some chagrin—about Hawk Mountain, many years past. The occasion was a luncheon in a posh fly-fishermen's club in London, where one of his English hosts talked at great length about the visit he had just made to Hawk Mountain and how famous the sanctuary was.)

One reason was the publication of Maurice Broun's book about the mountain, *Hawks Aloft*, in 1949, and the increasingly good press given "the world's first sanctuary for birds of prey"—always a catchy, if occasionally misleading phrase; some visitors expected to find the place swarming with nesting hawks, or at the very least a lot of hawks in cages. The road over the mountain was paved in 1950; electricity, and with it such amenities as hot water, came to Schaumboch's shortly afterward. The Brouns were regularly evening hosts to dozens of Hawk Mountaineers, and weekend overflows from the shelters often ended up on their back porch, particularly if it began to rain. They had made so many friends, Maurice began using a little space in his annual newsletter to thank the hundreds of people who sent them Christmas cards. The sanctuary was bustling most of the year. Only in the dead of winter did things really quiet down, and even then, after the road was blacktopped, winter visitors became more frequent. There was so much work to be done, and enough money in the kitty at last to afford it, that the sanctuary had an assistant curator; the position was filled, from 1953 on, by Alex Nagy.

But in all this bustle, which spoke for the success of the sanctuary, one matter remained outstanding that Maurice considered a failure, and that was the lack of legal protection given the hawks in Pennsylvania. He had tried, through writing articles and pamphlets and through the formal and informal lectures he often gave at the lookout (he referred to them as his "sermons on the mount") to influence hawk legislation everywhere. Visitors had gone back to their home states and campaigned for model laws to protect all hawks, and by the fifties this had begun to pay off. But not in Pennsylvania. In 1937, the state had protected all hawks except the Accipiters, which made the law meaningless, because when the game wardens weren't around—and sometimes even when they were—the hunters shot everything that passed, and not just hawks, but robins, too, and flickers and blue jays. Furthermore, the state itself continued until 1950 to encourage such indiscriminate shooting by offering the $5 goshawk bounty, which made every hawk a goshawk.

On good hawking days at the sanctuary, many of the birds of prey that sailed past were missing flight feathers or carried blood stains on their plumage, and people who loved hawks cringed at the thought of the carnage that must be going on that day farther east along the ridge. So Maurice took to leaving Hawk Mountain for a while on good hawking weekends and going to one of the shooting stands he knew about. There were six of them within 30 miles of the sanctuary—wherever a road crossed the ridge. If he were there, the hunters would take care to shoot only the birds they were quite sure were Accipiters. In the late forties, he began trying to interest people who visited Hawk Mountain to sacrifice a few days of pleasant company and quiet on the lookout in the fall and spend them at one or another of the shooting stands, to make sure the gunners only shot what was legal. Some of the members took him up on it, but for many the task seemed too unpleasant—not just watching the hawks being shot, but having to stand, unwelcome strangers, among a lot of rough coal miners carrying loaded shotguns. Maurice became impatient; it was his hope, he wrote in one newsletter, "that next fall local bird clubs and conservationists worthy of the title will cooperate with me in 'policing' these problem areas, and reporting all violations."

Such an effort, however, could only be stopgap, at best. The state had to change the law, or the passing birds at Hawk Mountain would continue to be battered survivors of a fusillade, and many would be shot west of the sanctuary after they had flown over it. "You'd get a good hawking weekend shaping up," Maurice said recently, "and everybody would be calling in and saying, 'How's the hawking, Maurice?' and I'd say, 'It looks *great*. You're going to have some real good hawking over the weekend.' But those nights I never slept, because I knew what was happening up the ridge. It just *killed* me. I had no pleasure out of the hawking. You could go up to Bake Oven Knob and stand by the side of the road, facing the east, in the direction of the oncoming hawks, and there'd be half a dozen guys lined up next to you with guns, shooting these birds as fast as they came. You'd see these hawks drop in the road, you'd see them drop in the woods; there was nothing you could do about it, because they'd always make sure to shoot sharpshins when I was there."

Maurice's angry needling of the Pennsylvania legislature, particularly the public needling in a national magazine, and the efforts of a group of Hawk Mountain regulars who called themselves the Pennsylvania Hawk Committee, finally spurred the state in 1957 to pass a law protecting all hawks—in the northeast corner of the state only, and only in September and October, an obviously grudging concession to those damned hawk lovers. It was quite a surreal experience, sitting on the lookout during the next dozen autumns, knowing that the hawks that came down the ridge were safe, but that if they drifted out beyond the Susquehanna River to the west—as they might well— they would be shot at.

And they were, the protected as well as the unprotected. Charley Thomas, sitting behind a glass-topped counter of his antique shop in Hamburg, remembers hawk shooting with a friend outside the forbidden area. "A shadow passed in front of me—I thought it was an airplane. Then I seen what it was, and it shot right over me. I didn't even lift my gun up." But downhill from him, his friend saw the huge bird overhead, fired first and asked questions later.

" 'Hey, Charley, come down here,' he says. 'I don't need to come down,' I said, 'and for Christ's sake stuff it in the rocks.' He says, 'What the hell is this?' He brought it up. I says, 'Jesus Christ, if there's a warden up here, that's a hundred bucks.' I says, 'Stuff it in the rocks, you killed a golden eagle.' And it was a mature bird—a beauty. When it came down—that time, there was still dead chestnuts standing—it broke a chestnut. It sounded like an airplane crashing."

When Maurice and Irma retired in 1966, the law remained the same. Not until three years later did the state finally pass a model hawk-protection law. Then, early in 1972, Mexico and the United States included birds of prey in their long-standing migratory bird treaty, which gave the protection of hawks—all hawks—the force of federal law. Hawks are still being shot; that remains a major cause of death among birds of prey. But the gunning has been reduced.

Gradually, over the years, many of the local hawk shooters made their peace with the Brouns, and some even went so far as to make their peace with the hawks. It helped that the sanctuary quickly brought economic benefits to the area. Various stores and a fruit farm appropriated the name Hawk Mountain to themselves. A tourist industry grew up with the sanctuary. And Maurice Broun's absolute certainty that what he was about was the only right course, and his persistence in selling that view, must have made a lot of people wonder whether they had been wrong about hawks. Early on, the one-time gunners began to show up at the gate on fine autumn days, smile— perhaps a little sheepishly—at Irma, who waited at the gate to take their small admissions fees, and then they went up to the lookout, just to watch. Occasionally, they took Maurice or one of the members aside and said they regretted their hawk shooting. This recanting still goes on. A local doctor recently told me that he had been "one of the damned fools who used to shoot hawks up there." That, he said with a shake of his head, had been before "we knew what we do now."

Charley Thomas admitted to having had run-ins with Maurice. "But we've gradually come to the point where the old hatred wore off. Today, I think he's a fine man. One man standing against the world—in a sense, you can't help but admire this." In Charley's case, perhaps part of the route to a man's heart lies through his child. Charley's daughter was introduced to the sanctuary as a Girl Scout; she became so attached to it, and to the Brouns, that eventually she had her wedding at Hawk Mountain, with the Brouns as witnesses.

Charley and the Brouns shared another thing in common—a love of the mountain itself. For Charley Thomas, the gravel-voiced hunter, this love had a mystic quality. "If I knew my time was coming," he said, "I would go up there and lay myself down, and let the deer patter over me."

FOUR

A slow day in mid-October. Warm and hazy, wind southeasterly—what there is of it. We have had eight days in a row of this, and the weather maps offer very little hope of change in the next week. Without a good wind to hold the birds to the ridges, most of them are slowly drifting south on a wide front, and those that are following the Kittatinny are leaving the main stem well to the east of the upper lookout and crossing the valley to the southern spur, then disappearing behind it, to coast along the southern face of the ridge after it zigs back to the west. What few hawks are passing the mountain are mainly flying over South Lookout or Owl's Head; we can see the silhouettes of a few people on North Lookout, but if a dozen hawks come near them today, they'll be doing well. The count is being taken here, on South Lookout, and at Owl's Head.

Until 1967, most of the counting of hawks was done from the North Lookout, the gunners' Point. But that was a really good observation spot only in a north to west wind, and—except in the broadwing season—when the wind got around into the south or east, very little went that way. Watchers found themselves constantly straining their eyes to pick out and identify hawks that were a mile off and cutting across the Kettle. In 1966, the sanctuary staff began experimenting to see just how many birds were being missed from North Lookout in this sort of weather. The telephone lines between the lookout and the entrance and Schaumboch's had been replaced by radios, and one man stationed himself with a walkie-talkie on the Observation Rocks while another worked his way southeast along the spur, checking in with the upper watch as he went, swapping notes on the visibility of the approaching hawks. Before long, the man on the spur got far enough away that he was picking up birds crossing the valley east of him that couldn't be seen from North Lookout. He continued to move along the escarpment, from one outcropping to the next, and finally ended on the crest of the first major headland down from the lookout, half a mile away. From there, one could see most birds that approached North Lookout along the main stem, if they stayed above the treetops; looking the other way, he could make out birds crossing as far off as Owl's Head, a mile away. In fact, the staff was astonished to discover that more than twice as many hawks actually passed the mountain on days like this one than could be seen with good optical equipment—or if seen, identified—from the traditional lookout. So the outcropping was cleared of several trees that obstructed the view and became South Lookout.

This is the best place to be today, but that isn't saying a great deal. We've had very few hawks so far—a couple of sharpshins and redtails, and one red-shoulder, in five hours. The wind is blowing barely enough to stir the leaves, and though that might be splendid during the broadwing migration in September, it produces the doldrums after the broadwings have gone by. No other birds are passing, either. Some poor hawking days are relieved by flights of geese and loons and jays and warblers and shore birds of one kind or another; more than 200 species of birds have been counted from the sanctuary, most of them migrating. One evening I sat on one of the outcroppings between here and the upper lookout and watched thousands upon thousands of robins beginning a long night's flight. Some were streaming over North Lookout; others passed over my head—one route heading west, the other southwest. I put my glasses on this flood from time to time and tracked back as far as I could see to the east, and there were always more robins. They were still coming when I left just before dark.

But there is nothing like that today. Sitting on the next rock is a lady from Ohio, who has never been here before and just picked up and drove several hundred miles earlier this week. She is profoundly disappointed. This is her third day of poor hawking, and she is—very sensibly, in view of the discouraging weather maps—planning to give it up and head home tonight. I am taking the count and collecting the admissions, and I am the only person around whom she can hold responsible for her frustration. She gets up from her rock, paces a bit, and says to me, "Hawk Mountain ought to be sued for false advertising."

I feel sympathetic, but I remind her that the sanctuary's literature cannot be construed as an advertisement for a sure thing. "No wind, no hawks" has been a warning broadcast in that literature since the 1930's. The trouble is that once Hawk Mountain became a well-publicized institution, the name conjured up images of hawks flying by, as Maurice Broun once put it, wing to wing. One reads the cautioning messages about the weather requirements, and then reads about the glorious days when hundreds of hawks go past, and tends to forget the first and expect the second. If you don't watch the developing weather approaching from the west, and come up here for a day or two, trusting to luck, you are very likely to be disappointed.

I've taken to visiting for a week or more at a stretch, figuring that at some point in there the weather will be perfect. But that doesn't always work, either. I drove down from Connecticut eight days ago, just as this southerly and easterly weather set in, and I plan to stay for four more, but it looks as if I won't see a brisk northwesterly day, or more than a smattering of hawks, the whole time.

I know how the lady feels. When I first began coming to the sanctuary, one of the main lures for me was the eagles. I had never seen an eagle. I was still working in New York City in those days, and my major birding trips were limited to weekends, so a crowd of us would rent a car, drive up early Saturday morning, and leave in the middle of Sunday afternoon—which is the way many visitors do it. We saw our share of hawks some days, but never an eagle. There's that standing joke up here, which must have sprung from a run of coincidences—eagle sightings on the hour: we speak of the two-o'clock eagle, the three-o'clock eagle, and so on. As Sunday afternoon drew on, those early weekends, some of my friends would start to agitate for departure, particularly if the hawking were poor. The die-hards among us would argue for staying until the three-o'clock eagle passed, and at 3:20 or so, when the agitation began again, we switched to the four-o'clock eagle. But no matter how late we stayed, we were disappointed. I hated to leave, each time. I *knew* that if we could stay a few more hours or a few more days we were bound to see an eagle. That was one reason I gave up visiting on weekends and ordered my life so that I could be here a week or more at a time. And the first time I did that—a friend and I spent eight days on the mountain in the middle of the broadwing season—we saw a bald eagle the first day, and a more or less two-o'clock eagle, at that.

Even on such a hawkless day as this, the sanctuary is beautiful. From here, the view is less spectacular than it is from North Lookout, because the wide valley to the north is hidden by the main stem of the ridge winding toward North Lookout. From the apex of the spur's angle at North Lookout, the land slopes gently, hugely down below us, spreads into the broad Kettle to our right, with the River of Rocks in the center and the long decline of the ridge's flank beyond. There has not yet been a frost, and the leaves have only just begun to turn this week—the black gums and the dogwoods becoming rose-colored, and some of the oaks and aspens and maples, pale yellow.

Here and there in the view are small bursts of spring green, tulip trees, which, on cloudy days, look like patches of sunlight on the hills' brown-green blanket. The cicadas and katydids saw and gossip in the Kettle; tiny black March flies swarm around the lookout; an occasional monarch butterfly bounces lightly by, idling south in the endless Indian summer. Overhead, the clouds hang almost motionless. No wind, no hawks.

A couple of other volunteers are taking the count at Owl's Head today. It's a small lookout—big enough for six people at the most—sitting at the top of a 100-foot slide of rocks. Few people go out there. Most days, posting oneself at Owl's Head is the Hawk Mountain version of self-exile in Siberia; when the wind is in the north or west and blowing hard, not many birds leave the main stem of the ridge and cross to Owl's Head, and though things improve there when the wind is in the south or east, relatively few birds pass the mountain those days anywhere. But it is quiet at Owl's Head; on weekends when the crowds swarm over the sanctuary, a few of the regulars retreat there, and since the sanctuary staff likes to have Owl's Head covered as often as possible, some volunteers will spend weekdays on the little lookout—as today. With the radio, South and "Unit One" keep each other company, and commiserate. Owl's Head isn't getting any birds, either.

One attraction of Owl's Head is the nearness of some of the passing birds. The cove between it and the Pinnacle at the end of the spur is a half a mile or so across, and a lot of the birds fly down the middle, but often a hawk or a group of hawks will strike the headland somewhat back of the lookout—toward South Lookout, in other words—and will turn back and coast around the corner, unaware until they are right on top of the lookout that there are people there. So they will pass within a few feet of the watchers, sometimes at eye level or a little below.

Because of that, I got an amazing look the other day at my favorite hawk, the red-shoulder—like the broad-wing, a Buteo, with a short tail and long, wide, rounded wings. In mid-morning, an adult red-shoulder slipped around the corner, close in and about 20 feet below us; it found a thermal out in front and rose on it. The sun was quite high on our right hand by then, and as the hawk sailed up toward the sun on its elevator—not 40 feet away from us—the light struck it perfectly, and the bird positively glowed: the cinnamon-orange shoulder patches in the black wings, and the white flecks in the wings and on the head and back, and the narrow white barring in the black tail all shone as if the bird had been burnished. Then, as it rose above us, it showed the lovely cinnamon feathering that covers the breast and belly and spreads out in the shape of a Y into the white underwings. No other hawk is more handsomely marked. We could be skunked the rest of the day and I would still count the day well-spent.

I very seldom see a red-shoulder in the Northeast except during migration. It can be a very hard bird to find once it has built its nest in swampy woods, because it isn't easily approached there; it doesn't soar a great deal unless it is courting and prospecting for a nesting site, and it prefers low perches, against the camouflaging fabric of the trees, when hunting or resting. Once you get to know its voice, that can be a considerable help, but the red-shoulder has a way of sounding off with a scream like that of a blue jay ("Often imitated by jays," say the field guides, probably giving the jay more credit than credit is due). William Brewster remarked in his journal about hearing a red-shoulder one September morning in 1892. "Its cries were quite as wild, ringing and exultant as in spring. The Blue Jay's imitation is certainly good but it never deceives me. It reproduces the form merely and lacks the essential quality of tone. This difference serves if the bird is near. If distant, I have only to remember that the Jay never utters more than three or four notes (usually but two) in succession, whereas the Hawk commonly repeats the cry from six to an indefinite number of times. It is decidedly the wildest sound to be heard in our Massachusetts woods."

I've only heard it once, so far as I know. The red-shoulder is becoming quite rare as a breeding bird in the Northeast, as it is in most of the country. When A. K. Fisher wrote his book on birds of prey for the Department of Agriculture, also in the 1890's, he said that from New England south "it is the most abundant breeder of any of the rapacious birds, and in Connecticut and the southern portions of New York it is safe to say that its nests outnumber those of all the other birds of prey combined."

It had replaced as most plentiful another of the Buteos, the red-tailed hawk. Maurice Broun's mentor, Edward Howe Forbush, remembered the redtail as "one of the common birds of my boyhood." They nested, he said, "in numbers over all New England wherever big timber grew. In the 60's and 70's of the nineteenth century we found their nests about the cities, even within city limits, and their wide wings wheeling in the summer sky were a common sight." Then the redtail declined as the timber was cut. The red-shoulder took over, and was still the commonest New England hawk, Forbush believed, in the 1920's, although by then there were signs of its having gone into a decline of its own. Now, in the Northeast, the redtail has regained primacy over the red-shoulder, and the broadwing, benefiting from the return of much farmland to the second growth forest it likes, is probably more numerous than either one.

The disappearance of the red-shoulder has sometimes been blamed on pollution of its environment by persistent pesticides and other poisons. The red-shoulder nests chiefly in wet woods and sometimes feeds quite heavily on frogs and toads and crawfish—as well as field mice—and this habit of feeding in swamps, often near farm territory, surely has led to the species picking up poisons that run off the farms into the swamps; and, of course, swamps have been sprayed directly for mosquitoes. But habitat change has probably also been a factor, just as it was in the red-tail's decline in the last century. John and Frank Craighead's study of raptor populations in Superior and Ann Arbor, Michigan, in the 1940's casts some light on this. In 1942, the red-shoulder was the most abundant species in their study areas, making up a third of the total population. Six years later, it was still predominant, but its percentage had dropped considerably. Meanwhile, the redtail was on the increase. The Craigheads suggested this might be a temporary shift, but they thought that it seemed significant that "it occurred simultaneously with drainage of swamps, cutting of woodlots, and generally more intensive farm practices, all of which reduced the habitat of the red-shouldered hawk, which prefers deep woods and swamps." The population of Buteos within the study area, they pointed out, was very regular: there were 53 in the nesting season of 1942, the same in 1948, and one less in 1949. Perhaps that indicated the "carrying capacity" of the area, they said, and as the red-shoulders diminished, the redtails quickly filled the gap. In any event, since then, the red-shoulder decline appears to have accelerated throughout the United States. And yet, at Hawk Mountain, the numbers of red-shouldered hawks counted each year have remained quite stable. Hawk Mountain may well have been counting, all along, mostly red-shoulders that came from wilderness areas in Canada still relatively untouched by man. No one knows.

Owl's Head is notable for its turkey vultures—what many people call buzzards. In the warm months of the year, there's a vulture roost near the base of the Pinnacle, across the deep cove, and another on the far side of the Kettle, where these big, dark brown carrion-eaters gather for the night. During the day, the updrafts around Owl's Head are apparently very attractive to them; they swing back and forth along the face of the headland, simply enjoying themselves in the air—the long wings held slightly above the horizontal, seldom flapping. Turkey vultures are certainly ugly enough, with their unfeathered heads—skin scarlet in the adults and black in the immatures. And on the ground they are clumsy looking and clumsy in fact. But on the wing, soaring, effortlessly riding the waves and ripples of air, tilting from side to side like tightrope walkers, they are all grace—and a pleasure to watch. As someone remarked years ago, "One might almost be willing to be a buzzard to fly like that."

The vulture usually looks black or dark brown in flight, but at reasonably close range one can see a triangle of silver gray along the underside of each long wing—the apex of the triangle at the back of the wing near the body, and the broad end at the tip. When the bird wheels in the sunlight, with the sun behind it and shining through the wings, this silver-gray turns to a glowing yellow—

completely unexpected the first time one sees it, and beautiful.

The turkey vulture, of course, is not generally thought of as beautiful. It has eating habits that most people consider unsavory. Its feet are so weak it is able to grab and kill only the most vulnerable of living prey, and it feeds mostly on the dead and the rotten. "When they find a dead animal," wrote one observer around the turn of the century, "they will not leave it until all (but the bones and other hard parts) has been consumed, and if it be a large one, or if it have a tough skin, they will often remain near it for days, roosting at night in the trees near by. After they have eaten—and sometimes they will gorge themselves until the food runs out of their mouths when they move—they will, if they are not too full to fly, roost in the nearest trees until their meal is partly digested and then commence eating again. Many times I have seen these birds in company with the black vulture [the turkey vulture's southern cousin] floating down a stream on a dead alligator, cow, or other large animal, crowded so closely together that they could hardly keep their balance, and followed by a number on the wing."

For many years, argument raged among ornithologists over whether or not turkey vultures could smell what they ate and whether the bird's sense of smell was well enough developed to allow it to depend on scent as well as its marvelous powers of sight in the search for food. Audubon was one who conducted experiments to find out, and he concluded that it could not; vultures didn't seem to be able to find a hidden carcass. But later researchers discovered otherwise, and the bird's ability to smell has in recent years been put to an unexpected use: leaks in natural gas pipelines can sometimes be found by looking for kettles of vultures, drawn to the spot by the rotten-egg smell, which is added to the gas for safety's sake. Probably they can smell food from quite a height, and not simply because of a sharp sense. Thermals boost more than air; a pilot-friend tells me he remembers flying along at several thousand feet and nearly being knocked out of the cockpit by a whiff of skunk.

The vulture seems to inspire marvelous writing. Edward Howe Forbush, for example, wondered how the vulture could smell anything but its own foul self—high with the stench of wallowings in putrid flesh—unless "the odor of a rotting carcass" was "an agreeable change."

One hawkwatcher says that he has been out at Owl's Head—alone and partly hidden behind a big boulder that stands as a kind of fort between the watcher and the precipice—and had vultures sweep by him not much more than an arm's length away. I imagine that would be rather a unique experience, since the turkey vulture has a wingspan of about six feet—in other words, as wide as I am tall. I haven't seen one quite that close, but the other day, a flock put on a remarkable show for us out there. It was the end of a long and practically hawkless afternoon. We had seen a few turkey vultures—"TVs," in hawkwatcher's shorthand—playing along the slope, but most of the local birds had been off foraging in their different directions. At about four, they began to head home. (It seems that certain levels of light, not an internal clock, bring the birds in; Alex Nagy was watching a recent partial eclipse of the sun from North Lookout, and as the moon moved across the sun early that afternoon, all the vultures flew home to roost, and then took off again when the sun was uncovered.) As usual in the evening, they hunted for a strong thermal near the roost on which they could congregate and wheel together before settling down for the night. This afternoon, the thermal they chose was right in front of us. Our own perch was then in shadow, but the first dozen or so of them to collect circled silently in sunlight close above us. Then, as the shadow rose slowly among them, there were 35, 40, at last 60 of them, swirling over our heads, some of them occasionally sliding out of sight behind the trees in back of us, then sliding into view again, the flock mixing and turning, each bird on its own path but all the slow ellipses and spirals within the same column of air. An evening dance, a community ritual. At last the birds turned and set, in a long, easy glide, for the roost at the base of the Pinnacle.

For many years, the sanctuary tried to keep a count of migrating vultures along with the other birds of prey, but finally that was given up. The birds from the local roosts, drifting back and forth along the ridge, made the counts unreliable. There have been as many as 160 vultures in the roost across from Owl's Head. They breed here, and then head south in the fall—presumably to avoid spending a winter on the mountain; but they start to return to the sanctuary in February, long before the winter is over. A few years ago, after the vanguard was back, 10 inches of snow fell one night, and then half an inch of freezing rain. The next morning, Alex drove past a roost and saw "several unfamiliar stump-like projections on the snow-covered ground." The stumps turned out to be seven vultures. Vultures on the ground is not an unusual sight; they feed there, and they even nest there. But these birds were obviously doing neither, and when Alex investigated, he discovered that they were covered with ice. Apparently they had perched in exposed situations overnight, and when they had tried to fly in the morning, they hadn't been able to get their wings open and had dropped like stones. Alex was able to brush the ice off three of them without pulling out any feathers, but he had to give the others a lift back to his house—four huge, frozen birds on the passenger seat beside him. "The vultures spent the night thawing in the garage," he said, "and then they were let go; they were last seen soaring east, over the Great Valley. . . ."

Down in the Kettle, below us on South Lookout, a group of Scouts or a school class is moving up the Copperhead Trail toward the ridge's crest. The shouts of the children rattle between the slopes, intruding on the soft silence of the long afternoon. "The object of this corporation shall be to establish and maintain preserves for the conservation of wildlife, and to provide means of educating the public in matters concerning wildlife." That declaration of educational purpose has been taken seriously here. Since the establishment of the sanctuary, heaven only knows how many young people—100,000?—have walked the trails and listened to lectures delivered on the trails or the lookouts or the lawn back of Schaumboch's or in the Common Room, with its displays of geology and trees, and its stuffed hawk specimens perpetually soaring beneath the rafters. Five thousand or more children come every year now in organized groups, and many others arrive with their families. There was once a nominal admission charge for the school and Scout groups, but a few years back the sanctuary—believing that that was where it should make a major investment—began admitting them all free. It also created a new assistant curatorship, for education.

The groups are often taken out on the trails by Jim Brett, who now fills that position. The gang below us sounds a little noisy, so it may be that he is not along on this trip. A stocky, pleasant biology teacher who used to bring his own school classes to the mountain for years before he joined the staff, Jim has invented an interesting lesson for teaching the general concepts of ecology. When he leads a group out along the Copperhead Trail, he carries with him a ball of string and a pair of scissors. He asks the students to join him in an experiment and has each of them, to start, choose something in the forest as a role to play; the idea is for the children to suggest possible connections between their roles. Between the one who chooses to be a robin and the one who chooses to be a tree, a line is tied; between the tree-child and the squirrel-child, another line; between the robin-child and the snake-child, still another; between the snake-child and the rock-child, another, and so on, until the children are standing at the points of a complicated web.

When Jim isn't along, there is a taped lecture, which can be used with a portable cassette player, by the students' regular teacher. A trail was developed especially for the purpose. The setting up of the trail and the use of tape recorders was one solution to a serious problem that has troubled the sanctuary for a number of years—overcrowding.

In the case of the children, a school class of 30 or a large Boy Scout group arrives at the mountain, often after a long, confining bus ride; when they flock up the mountain, exuberantly noisy in their escape from the bus, and like as not in a climbing race, you can hear them coming half a mile away. In the past, when they headed for the lookouts, they reached South first, overwhelmed it for a few minutes with scrambling and chatter, and then, prodded by their leaders, hurried on toward the upper watch. Whoever was in charge at South Lookout usually grinned and picked up the walkie-talkie to warn his opposite number on North, "A present is on the way," and all the adults seated on boulders within earshot of the radio groaned. Silence and space are two of the qualities that bring people to the sanctuary; as the children came within earshot, the silence was disrupted, the space shrank. Then the youngsters appeared at the brow of the lookout and swarmed down over the rocks, yelling to each other about the scenery or the hawks, completely oblivious to any hawkwatcher whose view they might block. When, after a quarter of an hour or so, they were collected for their departure, the hawkwatchers were grateful to see them go. It was an unfortunate confrontation. Serious hawkwatchers are normally delighted by the presence of a young person who might be introduced, during a few hours on the lookout, to the excitement of watching the passing hawks. Any one of these youngsters might catch the fever, if he or she were here alone or with a couple of friends. But in these big groups, the necessary quiet and concentration was impossible to come by. The students, in noisy shyness, herded by themselves and showed off to each other. And the adults' main concern, other than wishing the children would shut up and sit down or leave, was that as the youngsters scrambled over the rocks they would not fall and break a bone. On a Saturday or Sunday in particular, this scenario might be played out a dozen times, with little benefit to anyone.

So Jim laid out a series of study stations along a trail that led to a new lookout, east up the ridge, opened especially for such groups, and he taped his cassette lectures to be played on the trail, for those increasingly frequent days when there are too many of the groups on the mountain for him to see to himself.

Hawk Mountain has been a victim of its own success, in a way. In 1947, 4,000 visitors came to the sanctuary; these days, that many may pour through the gates on a single October weekend, and the two major lookouts will be jammed—"wall-to-wall people," as one veteran member put it. Maurice's book, newspaper and magazine articles, and television features have repeatedly broadcast word of the sanctuary across America and around the world. People who have been here and fallen in love with the place tell their birding friends, who visit and tell *their* friends. Thousands of people come here each year just for the view and the spectacular expanse of autumn foliage, and they, too, encourage others to do likewise. Since the late 1950's, despite its attempts to keep up with the crowds, the sanctuary has been bursting at the seams.

That chased the Brouns away. By 1959, the Hawk Mountain family they had done so much to nurture was too big to be dealt with as they had in the past. On top of that, the good road over the mountain attracted tourists who did not even know the sanctuary was here until they arrived. Old Schaumboch's, wrote Rosalie Edge, "standing close beside the road, is the focal point of all visitors. Not only is [it] thronged by Association members and other visitors, but lost travellers and motorists in distress seek assistance at all hours. Often the knock comes at the door at sunrise and frequently after midnight. Schaumboch's kitchen and living-room are filled with files and papers, books and other articles for sale—all part of the Sanctuary management, but certainly having nothing to do with the home life of the Curator and his wife."

Plans had been made to build the Brouns a residence well away from the road and to turn the inn into a headquarters office, but lack of funds delayed the start of the building. In 1960 the Brouns were offered the use of a member's home off the sanctuary; they accepted, and in 1963, they bought a place of their own, away from Hawk Mountain. From 1960 on, they were full-time residents at the sanctuary only in the dead of winter, when they could be assured their privacy would not be overwhelmed. They spent the weekends on the sanctuary, because of all that had to be looked after, but otherwise they went home at night. But even that arrangement didn't ease things sufficiently. On the weekends, Maurice dealt with hundreds and thousands of people—most of whom, it seemed, wanted a personal word with him—until he began to dread the weekends.

The intense, enthusiastic naturalist was being forced to become an expert in crowd management, and though he did it well, he hated it. Even the week nights were getting out of hand. He would tell Irma that he would be home at five, but just as he was closing up, an old friend or a curious tourist would collar him for a chat, and then another would appear—perhaps someone just down from the lookout, wanting to talk about the day's hawking—and then another. The long and the short of it was, he didn't get home until seven.

The pressures left a permanent scar. He is still the intense, enthusiastic naturalist. He strides around his farm, seeking, examining, cataloguing. A visiting friend is more than likely to be taken on a zigzagging tour of the place, Maurice pointing out bluebirds and vesper sparrows, cutting crosslots through his woods to check on his handsome paper birch—a rarity hereabouts—pausing to indicate and discourse on various species of ferns (he is an authority on the subject and has published an *Index to North Ameri-*

can Ferns) or a small patch of rattlesnake plantain or a cluster of mushrooms. He travels around the country, lecturing. It is clear that the out-of-doors and the cause of the environment have lost none of their hold on him. But for him, Hawk Mountain ultimately ceased to be a sanctuary in the truest sense of the word. And he is likely to say— doubtless recalling the way he drove himself when he was young, and the low pay available to conservationists, and the long, personally agonizing battle to save the hawks from gunning, and the paradox that his success at Hawk Mountain should change the sanctuary to something he could no longer bear—"The heartaches, that's all I remember of conservation." He remains curator emeritus, but he does not visit the sanctuary, and he does his fall hawking on weekdays, some distance up the ridge.

He and Irma retired in 1966. The cheery, heavy-set Alex Nagy stepped in. The curator's house was finally built, and Schaumboch's became the Headquarters. South Lookout was opened, not just to aid in the hawk counting but also to absorb some of the weekend crowds. The position of assistant curator for education was added. And still the sanctuary's popularity outdistanced its comfortable capacity. The parked cars of weekend visitors, bearing the license plates of all the New England states, New York, New Jersey, Delaware, Maryland, the District, Ohio, Illinois, a Canadian province or two, as well as Pennsylvania —regularly lined one side of the state highway for as much as a mile on either side of the entrance to the trail, sometimes 400 cars at once. A parking lot was built and others were planned. The trail to the lookouts was crowded not only with bird-club members and Boy Scouts in hiking boots but also with families in their Sunday best —including leather-soled business shoes and wobbly high heels—novice hikers gingerly but doggedly making their way over the stones. The tenting grounds were jammed by six o'clock every Friday evening, and the two Appalachian shelters, likewise. The lookouts were like beehives, with people sitting on every available rock, people moving from place to place, and everyone chatting.

Hawk Mountain, now officially a Registered Natural Landmark, is no different in this respect than many a state and national park: there are so many people who want to use it that it does indeed lose some of its sanctuary quality. And for a sanctuary that survives because of its members, that traditionally seeks personal contact with all its visitors, this presents an exceedingly troublesome dilemma. Is there a point at which people should be turned away? Should more facilities be built on the mountain? Should more lookouts be opened? Already, some of the regulars have unofficially opened the outcroppings on the escarpment between North and South Lookouts, particularly on weekends, to get away from the crowds. The association would not want to give up its scientific activities, such as the counting of hawks and other migrating birds; but what do you do if the distraction of the crowds becomes so great as seriously to interfere with the science? Which is more important—the hawk counting and the like, or the education in ecology one hopes goes on as new visitors crowd the mountain and are exposed to the spectacle of migration, the plants, the geology, and to people who are knowledgeable and excited about such things?

The youngsters out of sight below us make their way up the valley, then retreat. The afternoon wanes. Katydids converse tirelessly about Katy's guilt, crows call in the distance. There are no hawks, and likely there will not be for the rest of the day. The remaining watchers wait, as if the quiet had absorbed them: to my left, two women—friends who arrived together and chose rocks 10 feet apart; at the front, a young man in dungarees and a quilted brown jacket, his long hair bound behind by a rubber band; over near the trees on the right edge, a couple and their two children. Now and then, one of us raises binoculars to scan the ridge and the sky before us, but most of the time we just look out into the view. There is almost no talk, and for this moment at least it all seems very private.

FIVE

A light wind has been blowing steadily this afternoon, and we have had plenty of hawks to keep us occupied. A young bird artist joins us from one of the "middle look-outs" along the escarpment. "Well," he says triumphantly, "did anyone else see the peregrine?"

We all grimace in disappointment.

"Yeah," he says, "it came in real low, right over the tops

of the trees below us, and then zipped up in front of us—
went right over our heads. Beautiful. A mature female.
No one else saw it." The peregrine falcon is his favorite
bird. For that matter, because of its rarity here—or any
place else in the East—and the disastrous population collapse that has overtaken it, it is a favorite bird of every
hawkwatcher.

The first time I saw a peregrine, a friend and I were
standing at the marshy edge of a pond on the outskirts of
New York City. The bird—a fine, slate-blue adult—
appeared out over the water; as we followed it in the binoculars, it saw us and turned our way, flying slowly—
almost drifting—until it filled the field of view in the
glasses, so close as to be unnerving. The peregrine is about
the size of an average duck—15 to 20 inches long, with a
wingspan, pointed tip to pointed tip, of 3 to 4 feet, give or
take a few inches. That's a biggish bird. The purposeful,
fierce face—dark martial helmet with its dark side-pieces
that slashed down through the large eyes—glared at us
as if considering what action to take. Nervously, we lowered our glasses, and bird and birders studied each other,
while the falcon, hovering and gliding about 6 feet above
the water, continued to drift toward us until it was only 20
yards off. Then it turned and, driving, headed west.

A fit bird, I thought, to consider itself the equal of man.
Of all the birds of prey, the peregrine is the fastest and
most spectacular on the hunt. It towers up over its prey,
starts to dive, whips its wings a few times, then almost
closes them, falls, stirring the air behind it with slight mo-
tions of the wings. Some observers have wondered whether
it uses its wings in some way throughout the dive to increase its speed, for it has been estimated to stoop at speeds
of up to 275 miles an hour, but others think that the wings

(115)

probably move in mid-dive as rudders. In any event, people who have seen a peregrine dive say it is magnificent to watch. When it " 'stoops' from a great height upon its prey," wrote Edward Howe Forbush, "its plunge is so lightning-like that the bird seems to have been evolved out of a clear sky, and the sound of its rush is like that made by a rocket." It may strike its prey from above, or flatten out the dive, roll, and attack from the side, or stoop until it is below its flying prey, then pull out of the dive, roll on its back, and strike from below—always at tremendous speed. It may give chase in level flight and overtake a fleeing flock of sandpipers or blackbirds or ducks, or skim a river to pick off a sitting duck from behind. At the climax of the attack, the peregrine will hit with its talons, but often only to stun or kill, not to grab. Its feet are huge weapons; one common American name for the bird used to be great-footed hawk. The blow it delivers with its great feet is terrific; it can tear the side out of a snipe or snap the head right off a wooden duck decoy. After a mid-air strike, the falcon may double back and snatch its cartwheeling victim as it falls, or watch the prey tumble to the ground before dropping on it and breaking its neck.

Peregrines have a reputation for boldness. Frank M. Chapman—whose field guide was the birder's bible until Roger Tory Peterson's book replaced it—remarked that when he was out shooting snipe he had seen peregrines "dart down to rob me of wounded Snipe lying almost at my feet, nor did my ineffective shots prevent them from returning." As I say, a fit bird to consider itself the equal of man.

In one respect, the peregrine has particular right to consider itself man's equal: very occasionally, it kills not for the food but—so it seems—for sport. Some observers have expressed disgust at, as one man put it, this "lust of slaughter." The falcon will put up a flock of sandpipers or herons and dash through it, striking out to one side and the other; the herons or sandpipers fall, the falcon speeds on.

But though they may kill in sport rarely, far more often they sport without killing. They are not infallible hunters, certainly, but many of their misses seem to be intentional. A peregrine will bully flocks of birds—scare them up and then fly right through their midst without touching a one. William Brewster described a male peregrine chasing a duck: after "glancing close past and well in advance of her, with amazing velocity, he wheeled and hovered directly in her path, yet refrained from using, or even displaying, his sharp talons when she passed within easy reach of him." Another watcher saw a peregrine play tag—force a cormorant to dive from a great height and stay just behind it all the way down to the water until, a few feet above the surface, the falcon put on a little extra speed, overtook the cormorant, "tapped [it] lightly on the back, then circled easily away. . . ."

It is a bird to stir the imagination—dashing, agile, powerful, a very rocket of a bird, indeed, and just unpredictable enough in behavior to give it at least the appearance of being able to reason, to outthink its quarry.

One also associates the peregrine with topographic grandeur. It breeds in many parts of the world (only the osprey and the raven have comparably widespread populations), and it may nest flat on a bog in Finland, on the tundra in the Arctic, in a cut on a river bank in Alaska, in the top of a tree in Germany, or in a church steeple in Great Britain; but, typically, it makes a scraped-out nest on a ledge, high on the face of a cliff overlooking a broad river valley. It returns to that ledge, or one near it, year after year, and the eyrie is passed from one generation to the next, in a remarkable continuity. On the island of Lundy off the coast of Wales, once a pirate hangout, there is an eyrie that was known as early as 1243. For that matter, says British scientist Derek Ratcliffe, of the 46 nest ledges in the British Isles which falconers knew about between the sixteenth and nineteenth centuries, all but four were occupied by peregrines in the period 1930 to 1939. An eyrie may be vacant for years and then be reoccupied. It is as if the spot itself called to the passing peregrine—and it may do just that. When the ledge is occupied, the birds create a streak of white on the cliff face by excreting over the side, and this acts as a telltale—at least to ornithologists looking for eyries. Once the place has been abandoned for a while, bright-colored algae or lichen colonize the fading white streaks, as well as other places below the eyrie where nitrogen-rich detritus has been washed down by rain. If there is a ledge below the nest ledge, the grass there grows especially thick and green. One student of the bird has suggested that these streaks of vegetation not only tip off the peregrine watcher to the location of an ancient nesting place, but also tip off other peregrines.

It is against the backdrop of these river-valley cliffs—used by peregrines for as long, perhaps, as the cliffs existed—that during the breeding season the peregrine's mastery of its element is most breathtaking.

Joseph A. Hagar has written about it. After Massachusetts passed its hawk-protection act in 1934, the Division of Fish and Game assigned him to keep watch over the eyries in the Commonwealth (there were 14 of them, Hagar discovered) and protect them from the hands of falconers and egg collectors. So for a number of years, Hagar had an unparalleled opportunity to observe the falcon's behavior.

Here, in a contribution to Arthur Cleveland Bent's *Life Histories*, he describes a displaying male: ". . . again and again the tercel [or tiercel, so-called, originally by falconers, because the male is usually about a third smaller than the 'falcon,' or female] started well to leeward and came along the cliff against the wind, diving, plunging, sawtoothing, rolling over and over, darting hither and yon like an autumn leaf until finally he would swoop up into the full current of air and be borne off on the gale to do it all over again. At length he tired of this, and, soaring in narrow circles without any movement of his wings other than a constant small adjustment of their planes, he rose to a position 500 or 600 feet above the mountain. . . . Nosing over suddenly, he flicked his wings rapidly 15 or 20 times and fell like a thunderbolt. Wings half closed now, he shot down past the north end of the cliff, described three successive vertical loop-the-loops across its face, turning completely upside down at the top of each loop, and roared out over our heads with the wind rushing through his wings like ripping canvas. Against the background of the cliff his terrific speed was much more apparent than it would have been in the open sky. The sheer excitement of watching such a performance was tremendous; we felt a strong impulse to stand and cheer."

Many men have felt that way about a peregrine's performance. European falconers traditionally thought of it as nobility's bird. The *Boke of St. Albans* in 1486 ranked the eagle as the bird fit to hunt with emperors, and the gyrfalcon as the bird of kings, but on the whole kings and emperors were every bit as fond of the peregrine as were the princes and dukes and earls to whom the peregrine was assigned in the medieval reckoning. William the Conqueror's Domesday Book, an early nineteenth-century survey of the estates of England, mentions a number of specific peregrine eyries, presumably as assets of the estates in question. Peregrines were given as ceremonial gifts; in 1335, for example, the king of Scotland sent one to King Edward III in London. And rent for the Isle of Man was a pair of peregrines, paid to the crown by the Dukes of Atholl at each coronation of a new sovereign.

Peregrines trained to hunt with man were particularly esteemed for their spectacular flights—the ringing-up, or spiraling, after a climbing heron (herons were often the prey the females were trained to hunt, and the word "handsaw" in the expression "he can't tell a hawk from a handsaw" is said to be a corruption of "heronshaw," "hernshaw," and "henshaw," old names for the heron; in the age of chivalry, a man who didn't know the difference between a hawk and a heron was certainly a dull fellow), the waiting-on, high over the falconer's head, until the hounds sniffed out the prey for the falconer to force into the open, the sudden lightninglike stoop after the victim, the hawk's acrobatics as a fleeing grouse or snipe dodged and dived beneath it, the act called "throwing-up," as the prey dove steeply into cover, the hawk staying with it until the last split second, when it pulled sharply out of the dive and streaked upward to wait on again.

The peregrines used in falconry were either taken from the nest as eyasses (a word for the unfledged birds, from the French *niais*, or "nestling"), or were caught near the nest soon after the first flight, but before they could fly well, or were trapped as adults, usually on migration— "passage" birds on their first flight south and "haggards" or adults that had flown free for a year or more. There were elaborate setups for trapping migrating falcons (and goshawks, too), notably in the lowlands that arc down through Holland and along the French coast to Spain, where the passing hawks were concentrated. The Dutch, in particular, built this into a thriving industry that also included the making of equipment for falconry—the bells worn by the hawks, jesses for their legs, hoods, and so on. The remnants of that industry still existed until the start of the Second World War.

Eyass peregrines were generally thought to be inferior hunters as compared to passage birds that had flown wild for a while and learned to fend for themselves. Nonetheless, many falcons were taken from the nest before they flew. Other depredations on peregrine nests were the result of a science called oology, which attained the status of a fad in the last century; hundreds of thousands of bird eggs, including large numbers of peregrine eggs, were stolen from nests by thousands of amateur and professional collectors. But the peregrine survived well. When a whole clutch was stolen, the pair normally started another right away. The loss of young birds from the nest seemed to be compensated for by the existence of a surplus of adult birds; there was some depth to the population. When a falconer trapped an adult, or a hunter shot one during the breeding season, that same surplus provided a replacement, sometimes within hours (for example, a young female appearing at the eyrie and settling down to brood eggs she had not laid but knew how to care for as well as the dead parent).

Falconry—no more than the falcons themselves—has never been very popular in the United States. Most of the effect of falconry here has been caused by the many people who were not falconers at all, who wanted not to train hawks for the hunt or to go to the trouble of flying their birds regularly to keep them healthy, but simply to own one of these regal birds as a fancy pet. As often as not, such people haven't the vaguest idea of how to keep their birds in good condition. Among the sick birds brought to the sanctuary's "hawk hospital" are victims of poor care by the ignorant. A painful example was the kestrel brought in with its beak filed down to make it less dangerous and its tail feathers and long wing feathers cut short so that it would fit in a small cage. In such tragedies, the true falconers can be blamed only for creating jealousy—by having working partnerships with these handsome wild creatures.

Now, however, a great debate goes on concerning falconry; with many birds of prey declining in numbers, should anyone be permitted to "harvest" them? There is a concerted effort being made in some American conservation quarters to prevent the falconers from capturing any more wild birds, particularly peregrines; that species is believed to be in serious trouble, though mostly for reasons other than falconry, to be sure.

But that is a modern development. By the time America was colonized, guns had been invented, and falconry had declined from a way of life to an exotic hobby; it was a lot less trouble to load and shoot a gun than train and care for and hunt with a hawk. Furthermore, Americans saw themselves as doing battle with the wilderness, and all wild things were viewed either as enemies in that battle or as sources of food. So a "practical" view of the peregrine prevailed in this country, and the bird got a very mixed press.

Alexander Wilson's friend George Ord, who edited and annotated and augmented Wilson's *American Ornithology* when it was reprinted in the middle of the nineteenth century, called the peregrine a noble bird, but Audubon described peregrines as pirates and gluttons. He noted that the "French and Spaniards of Louisiana have designated all the species of the genus Falco by the name of '*Mangeurs de Poulets*' "—and, indeed, the occasional depredations of the peregrine on the chicken yard was one reason for its mixed press. Audubon, however, suggested that a more accurate name for the species would be *Mangeurs de Canards* because peregrines so often fed on ducks—in fact, a great deal more often than they ate chickens. Ultimately, Americans did take to calling it the duck hawk. But their attitude toward it did not change. Even A. K. Fisher, in his pioneering study in 1895 for the Department of Agriculture, concluded that it is "fortunate for the poultry-raisers that the species is comparatively rare throughout our country," that the "Duck Hawk is one of the few birds of prey in whose favor little can be said." It was a view based on agriculture, first, and on a man-centered morality—what the peregrine did, supplying its food, was robbery and murder.

So, although the peregrine in America did not suffer greatly from the depredations of falconers, there was an attitude—an agriculturalist's and gunner's and moralist's attitude—that dictated killing the bird, disturbing its breeding, stealing and killing its young. And the oology bug was as virulent here as it was in Europe. For example, there were some 20 known eyries in Vermont during the 1920's, possibly a few more than that by the next decade; between 1920 and 1934, 53 sets of the handsome, cream-colored, chocolate-marked eggs were stolen from these few nests. At one famous eyrie in Massachusetts, it has been said, at least 49 sets of eggs were collected between 1864 and 1931, and some seasons the resident pair relaid twice and still was not permitted to brood a clutch to hatching. It was reported in the 1880's that on one day 30 egg collectors climbed to the eyrie.

The remarkable thing—in Europe as here—was that although some eyries were eventually abandoned because there were no replacements to take over when the parent birds died, even so the species showed an ability to sustain itself and rebound from such losses. That beleaguered Massachusetts eyrie, for one, continued to be occupied season after season. And when ornithologist Joseph J. Hickey organized 147 fellow birders in 1942 to take a census of the North American peregrines east of the Rockies, they found 275 active eyries.

Joseph Hagar felt like standing and cheering as he watched the tiercel perform in front of its cliff in the 1930's. Nowadays, simply the appearance of a peregrine —anywhere in eastern North America—is enough to make one stand and cheer. This species, which used only thirty years ago to breed from Nova Scotia to Alabama, no longer nests in the East at all—at least, no one has found an active eyrie in the last ten years—and the only peregrines to be seen anywhere in the region are migrating birds from the north and east of it. I, who was growing up around Boston when Joseph Hagar was looking after his 14 eyries, never made the trip to the western part of the state to see one of them. Having survived the shooting and the egg collecting and the pet keepers and the falconers for centuries, the birds have vanished within my lifetime. Occasionally I see a peregrine on its migration between Canada or Greenland and South America, idling along over some salt marsh at 50 miles an hour and scaring up every wader and shore bird on the premises, and I have seen three, I think, passing Hawk Mountain, which records a dozen or two dozen of these birds in a fall. But there is no place in the East—in fact, few places in the entire continental United States—where I could go now to see what Hagar described. Even the western segment of the peregrine population is doing badly, and an Alaskan population, which only a few years ago was thought to be holding its own, is now on the skids. The peregrine has been nearly wiped out in this country—partly by the disturbance caused by more people looking for more places to hike, rock-climb, picnic; partly by robbery from the nests; partly by illegal shooting; partly by highway construction in what used to be wild and isolated areas; partly, no doubt—at least in some situations—by a diminishing food supply; but many scientists believe the most important factor, the reason that the peregrine population has collapsed so precipitously in the last three decades, is that persistent pesticides and other pollutants have disrupted the bird's reproductive system.

Ironically, as the population collapse occurred, the peregrine became a major instrument through which the biologists and ornithologists began to discover the extent and the nature of the impact these chemical compounds have on birds, particularly birds of prey.

The problem is breeding failure, not just by a pair here and there, but most or all of the peregrines in wide geographical areas. A decline in peregrine populations was noticed first in Germany, in about 1946. That same year, in Massachusetts, it seemed to Joseph Hagar that his peregrines produced a bumper crop of young; in the following summer, however, some sort of disaster struck, and Hagar observed a phenomenon he'd never seen before in all his years of watching eyries: there were broken eggs in a good many of the scrapes. The same thing was noticed in Quebec in the spring of 1948, and one observer there saw a weird scene: a peregrine eating one of its own eggs. By 1951, some of the Massachusetts eyries were unoccupied. In 1953, scientists in Finland became aware that something dreadful was happening to the Finnish population of the peregrine, and two researchers in New York, who had been studying the eyries of the Hudson River shore for a number of years, saw a complete nesting failure at all of them, for the second year in a row. The next summer, Hagar could find no active eyries and only scattered single birds in Massachusetts. The Finnish observers estimated that in 1958 their peregrine population was down to 10 per cent of what it had been. In Germany, in Great Britain, the collapse was not yet so drastic as that, but it was nonetheless severe.

The peregrine was failing to reproduce. Birds would pair off but not nest; some would nest, but later than normal; eggs were being abandoned; eggs were breaking in the scrapes, or vanishing, leaving behind only bits of shell or nothing at all—and the strange thing about that was that birds that would normally have laid a second clutch right away if they lost an entire clutch just didn't.

For some while, the individuals who were watching this happen thought it was only occurring in their own bailiwicks, and they tried to explain it by what they could see —some local increase in egg-eating predators such as raccoons, or bad weather, or human disturbance, or a failing food supply. A precipitous collapse of a species, on both sides of a great ocean, was unheard of, and though there was talk at the International Ornithological Congress in 1962 that not a single peregrine pair in the eastern United States had succeeded in bringing off young that year, even that report was received with skepticism.

It fell to Derek Ratcliffe in Great Britain and Joseph Hickey in the United States to stir the rest of the scientific community to a recognition of the scope of the problem.

The British experience was particularly interesting. During the war, an attempt had been made in England, especially in the south, to exterminate peregrines, because it was thought that they were likely to prey on carrier pigeons and so interfere with the war effort. Thus, at the end of the war, as far as anyone could tell, there were no peregrines left in Cornwall, for example, and only one pair in Dorset. But some ten years later, those two counties had 25 breeding pairs between them. Obviously the bird was as resilient as ever, and there had been enough surplus in the population to supply replacements for empty eyries; it was just what one might have expected.

Then, in the late 1950's, the recovery stopped, and reversed. As elsewhere, there was marked reproductive failure. Derek Ratcliffe worked for the British Nature Conservancy, and in 1963, largely at his urging, the British Trust for Ornithology sponsored a nationwide study of the peregrine, to which 170 Britons contributed their observations of breeding birds that year; Ratcliffe collated and published the findings, which showed that the situation of the peregrine in Great Britain was indeed serious. Ratcliffe also approached the matter from another angle. These broken eggs in the nests—the shells looked thinner than they ought to be, actually fragile. Were they in fact thinner? He compared the eggs in museum and private collections with recent clutches and discovered two things: not only were the recent eggs on the whole much thinner-shelled—say 15 or 20 per cent thinner—but also the thin eggshells had begun to appear with remarkable abruptness in about 1946 and 1947. The same peregrine's eggs would be of normal thickness one season, and a year later would decline sharply.

Meanwhile, in the United States, Joseph Hickey had organized a project to explore the breeding territory he had covered in his 1942 study. Two of his colleagues set out to check, in person, the breeding status of the peregrine in eastern North America. Starting in Georgia in April 1964, they worked their way north and northeast, mainly searching the Appalachians, and ended in June in Nova Scotia and New Brunswick. They knew of 236 spots that were well-enough documented to be considered traditional eyries. Some were already known to have been long abandoned, and some were overly difficult to reach or to find. But including the sites checked on by other birders, 146 eyries were investigated that summer, plus a good deal of promising-looking territory along the way. "Our efforts," they reported, "failed to find a single occupied cliff. At best, by estimating the age of excreta on cliffs, we found signs of recent occupancy, say within the last two years, at perhaps five or six eyries." They did not conclude that, Q.E.D., there were no peregrines breeding anywhere in eastern North America, but their findings did show that even if there were a few peregrines still around, a population that had numbered perhaps more than 600 in 1942— including the surplus, the potential breeding replacements—was in 1964 very close to zero.

Next, following up Ratcliffe's eggshell measuring in Great Britain, Hickey and his colleague Daniel W. Anderson measured North American eggshells, and they got strikingly similar results to Ratcliffe's. The dates for the collapse on both sides of the Atlantic were more or less identical, and the eggshell-thinning had appeared suddenly the same years. Something very strange was happening.

And while all these discoveries were being made about the peregrine, observers were also noting similar breeding troubles in other birds of prey—particularly the bald eagle and the osprey in North America, and the golden eagle and the British sparrow hawk (close cousin to the sharpshin) in Great Britain. Marked declines in those species had also begun at about the same time and involved the very same symptoms—thin shells, some egg eating, egg breaking, odd breeding behavior.

The pieces of the puzzle were at least beginning to be sorted out. The extent of the problem finally became generally known, thanks to a Working Conference on Birds of Prey and Owls held in France in 1964, an Audubon conference on the bald eagle the following year, and an international conference on the peregrine held at the University of Wisconsin late that summer.

But what was causing the problem? The scientists thought they knew at least one direction in which to look —the pesticides and pollutants with long lives in the environment, particularly organochlorine pesticides. As Ratcliffe noted, the evidence pointed to some "widespread and pervasive environmental change," taking place about 1945–47. Radioactive fallout wasn't a likely culprit; the changes in eggshell thickness followed distinct geographical patterns—very noticeable thinning in one area, none in another—which matched a "developing regional pattern of contamination by chemical pollutants during this period." There were, for example, the polychlorinated biphenyls, or PCBs, used in various manufacturing processes and then dumped into the atmosphere in smoke. Their use had boomed after the world war. And there was the sudden heavy application of organic insecticides and herbicides and fungicides after 1945; the introduction of the first of these—DDT—into general use about 1945 and 1946, "coincided closely," Ratcliffe noted, "with onset of the eggshell change."

By the 1960's, it had been known for some time that DDT and its brethren among the persistent organochlorine pesticides had potentially dangerous side effects to go along with the immediate benefits they offered. They were "wide-spectrum" compounds; that is to say, you might spray DDT to kill mosquitoes or spruce budworms and end up killing not only what you wanted to kill, but also a great many other things as well—beneficial insects, birds, fish, mammals. And they were called "persistent" with reason; they had long lives in the environment, and sometimes retained their potency for years. They also lent themselves to a concentration effect. They were not very soluble in water, but they were soluble in fat, so if they were eaten, the body of the feeder tended to absorb them rather than passing them out of the system. That set up a process in which one of these pesticides would, for example, be sprayed on a marsh or a lake, in very low concentrations, say to control biting insects, and the smaller organisms would take in the poisons until they carried a more potent concentration in their systems than was in the water; these small animals and plants would be eaten by larger ones, which would be eaten by still larger ones, and so on up the food chain, at each step up the predator species storing greater amounts of the pesticides until at the top of the chain a fish might be carrying these poisons in doses thousands of times—even millions of times— stronger than the concentration in the water. At these levels, they might well pose a danger to the health of the fish and the health of any creature—such as the osprey or the bald eagle or the double-crested cormorant—that depended on the fish for food.

In the case of the peregrine, the concentration process would load the ducks and herons and shore birds the falcon fed on. Ratcliffe supposed that in some way the eggshell-thinning—which could lead to eggs being broken just by the weight of the brooding bird—was caused by a disturbance of the female bird's metabolism, and that this disturbance was the product of the chemicals the birds were eating in their food.

The cause could lie somewhere else, of course. At the peregrine conference in Wisconsin in 1965, the participants went to great lengths to consider every other possibility they could think of for the population collapse: human disturbance, changes in climate, failing prey populations, some sort of epidemic. Reading the proceedings of that conference (which were published by the University of Wisconsin Press in 1969 as *Peregrine Falcon Populations*), one gets the distinct impression that many of the participants were bending over backward, trying not to reach hastily the conclusion most of them thought was the right one—not just out of scientific caution, but from a consciousness that if they did reach the conclusion that persistent pesticides were a major cause, they were certain to be assailed as anti-Man, anti-Progress, and anti-American. Hadn't the pesticides been a great help in controlling disease all over the world, and weren't they essential to growing food for the burgeoning population? Rachel Carson had been vilified as a Cassandra in tennis shoes by the pesticides industry since the publication of *Silent Spring* in 1962; indeed, such vilification was aimed at any scientist who took the same ground. No one in the Establishment was very likely to be grateful for a new attack on the persistent pesticides, however justified the attack might be. In fact, a restatement of the problem by scientists would probably decrease their credibility as scientists; what was expected of them in the community at large was some sort of painless solution.

And if poisons were to blame, some more convincing proofs than chronological coincidence and geographical correlations were needed. At the Patuxent Wildlife Research Center, operated in Maryland by the US Bureau of Sport Fisheries and Wildlife, two researchers began to study what happened when two of the persistent organochlorine pesticides—DDT and dieldrin—were fed in small doses to American kestrels, the handsome little cousins to the peregrine. (Here, as in all inquiries of this sort, investigators were limited to using as subjects only those species that could be fairly easily induced to breed in captivity, such as mallards, quail, pheasants, doves, cowbirds, and kestrels.) They discovered that small doses of DDT and dieldrin did produce marked eggshell-thinning. Also, the effects were cumulative, one generation to the next: the dosed offspring of dosed parents laid even weaker eggs and had poorer breeding records than their parents. That might help to explain why a drastic population decline didn't occur in some places until years after thin eggshells began to appear.

A number of subsequent experiments in laboratories, coupled with observations in the field, substantiated these findings and elaborated on them. DDT and DDE—a compound produced as DDT slowly breaks down— each produced thin eggshells and decreased fertility, and more than the normal numbers of hatchlings died before they grew old enough to fly. (By some estimates, there are millions of pounds, perhaps a billion pounds, of DDE drifting around in the world's environment now.) Dieldrin thinned eggshells, too, and seemed to delay the breeding cycle. The PCBs cast off by industry might or might not thin eggshells somewhat, but, more important, they killed embryos and slowed up the breeding process. In general, the higher the organochlorine residues found in eggs and the birds that laid them, the thinner the shells. In addition, some of these poisons had severely toxic effects on adults, and if the birds got enough of the stuff in their brains they went into convulsions and died. That was most likely to happen when the bird suffered some sort of stress— illness, sometimes, or most likely starvation; if the bird began living off its fat, that could release enough of the stored poison into the system all at once to kill it.

So that was where the problem began, with accumulated toxic chemicals in the system. Not all species of birds reacted the same way to the same poisons. In fact, it seemed that not all individuals in any one species reacted the same. But the general picture was conclusive. The next question was, how did such toxic pollutants in the birds' systems produce the observed effects on reproduction? Scientific investigation and the publication of research papers are so segmented and specialized now that a clue existed in print for some time before the key article was discovered by people interested in avian reproduction. The authors of the article had been studying the effects of drugs in rats; specifically, how fast the rats burned up hexobarbitol (a sleeping potion) if their food was held back. The results of this experiment were reasonably uniform for a while, and then suddenly in one of the tests the rats, having been dosed, woke up much sooner than they had been doing. The researchers mistrusted the result; something must have been different about that particular test. They went over it step by step, but found it had been normal. Then was there something peripheral to the experiment that might have affected the result? There is where they found the one thing different: the rats' cages had been sprayed with chlordane, one of the organochlorine insecticides. Following that lead, the researchers discovered that chlordane had the effect of stimulating a rat's liver to overproduce an enzyme that broke down the sleep-inducing drug so that it could be passed out of the system. And chlordane didn't have this effect just on hexobarbitol in the rats; the enzyme it stimulated broke down a lot of things, including—as Cornell Professor David B. Peakall noted pointedly in an article on the discovery—the sex hormones, estrogen, testosterone, and progesterone.

That opened up a lot of possibilities. If organochlorine pesticides did the same thing to birds they did to these rats, that meant that the entire chemistry of the breeding cycle could be affected, which might explain all sorts of puzzling things: the late laying, the thin eggshells, the disinterest in laying at all, the egg eating, the failure to start second clutches, and so on. At Cornell, Peakall and his colleagues tried an experiment with ringdoves. They were particularly interested in what effect DDE had on the ability of the female bird to draw upon stores of calcium in her system to form eggshells—an event that takes place just before the eggs are laid. They found that DDE apparently slowed down the activity of an enzyme that the bird had to have in order for the calcium to be delivered to the oviduct.

The scientific community is not yet sure that that is the whole answer; there has been speculation that the problem may really lie with the pesticides' effect elsewhere in the system. In any case, it is quite clear that Derek Ratcliffe's hunch was right: in one way or another the metabolism of birds, and particularly the sexual system, can be severely disrupted by these pollutants.

Aside from the implications this may have for man—and there are some scientists deeply concerned about it, some not—the persistent pesticides, and probably PCBs as well, have had a serious effect on those birds that operate at the top of long, cumulating food chains—including, in the United States, not just a number of eagles and hawks but also herons, egrets, petrels, cormorants, and pelicans.

And the organochlorines are not the only damaging pollutants. Heavy metals, particularly lead and mercury, as well as oil, are thought to present their own hazards. And since in all likelihood the birds don't take in just one poison at a time but eat food that contains unpredictable mixes of DDE, DDT, lead, PCBs, and so on, the picture is not only scarifying but complicated and confusing. Some investigators also think there is a chance all the potential poisons—perhaps some of the worst ones—haven't yet been identified. Stanley Wiemeyer, one of the Patuxent researchers who did that first study of the effects of DDT and dieldrin on breeding kestrels, has recently been keeping track of an osprey population on the Potomac River. When I talked to him, his ospreys seemed to be declining, though not so drastically as ospreys farther to the northeast. "Frankly," he said in a gloomy tone, "I can't tell you *what* is doing it. The tests we've made for residues in this situation aren't very conclusive. It may be something we're not even testing for yet."

Even so, the evidence seems to indicate that when use of persistent pesticides stops, the decline in some birds of prey stops. Gradually the accumulated poisons are burned out of their systems and cease to interfere with the breeding process. Populations may even recover: the use of dieldrin in sheep-dips was prohibited in Scotland, and the reproductive success of golden eagles—which are known to feed on the carcasses of sheep—shot up again. The same sort of thing appears to have happened, as soon as DDT use diminished locally, to some osprey colonies in the American Northeast.

On the other hand, the organochlorine pesticides have spread all over the world now, in wind and rain and sea water and, perhaps most important, in billions of living creatures. DDT may never again be used heavily in the United States, but other, poorer nations feel forced to continue, to control disease and crop pests; the spread of the residues to all corners of the earth will go on, and North American birds that breed where little or no DDT has been used will continue to pick it up—as Arctic-breeding peregrines do now—from their prey there and in wintering territory in South America. In the United States and elsewhere, others of the organochlorine pesticides continue to be used, and a number of them are in some respects more potent than DDT. And other sorts of pollution go on undiminished.

Furthermore, once a breeding population drops to very low levels, the species' situation becomes exceedingly precarious. A simple thing like bad weather during a few consecutive nesting seasons—which can wipe out eggs and young, but which under normal circumstances the population would compensate for with its surplus—may eliminate the species from wide stretches of territory. And recovery is not enhanced by such forms of environmental disruption as highway building, mushrooming suburbia, the draining of wetlands, the disposal of mountains of trash and sewage, the noise of blasting and trucks and jets, the "taming" of the wilderness for the use of a constantly growing public in search of recreation—all habitat disturbance on a grand scale.

Things may get better, of course. Governments are at least becoming aware of the extent of the environmental problem. But for the last ten years, the watchers at Hawk Mountain have felt at times as if they presided at a wake. Through the medium of the birds, one sees what is happening to the natural world in which—ignorant of it or not—man must exist. And one sees creation slowly rescinded, bits and pieces of the world's art being whittled away.

A few years ago, a large falcon appeared out in front of the North Lookout, coming at us head-on. The watcher who spotted it called out in a tone that said *look sharp, everyone,* "Falcon—over Three!" As it approached, the level of excitement on the lookout rose rapidly, and from one side and then the other came what might be called anticipatory cheers: "It's a mighty big bird." "Look how flat the wings are." "Look at that face." And finally, *"Peregrine, by God!"* Usually a peregrine passing North Lookout breaks away from the spine of the ridge before reaching the hawkwatchers and speeds past several hundred feet out to the north. But this bird, *rara avis* indeed, made only a feint in that direction, and then turned to drift directly over the lookout, and the watchers greeted it with a burst of applause.

On one late September afternoon, a bald eagle glided over the ridge toward us, circling slowly every few hundred yards, putting on a tremendous show, and gradually slid down to a perch for the night on the mountainside before us. The bald eagle, too, is a species whose marked decline in the East has been anxiously watched. This one hadn't "gone through," as the saying is at the sanctuary, so it wasn't counted in that day's totals. The next morning, a lot of us got to the lookouts earlier than usual, just to see the eagle again.

Certainly, everyone knows that Ben Franklin thought the bald eagle a poor choice as the national bird; it was, he said, a creature of "bad moral character." He would have preferred the wild turkey as an emblem. But it seems to me that Franklin cannot have known the eagle very well. Granted, the turkey is a bird of good moral character, eats only acorns and the like, and provided early Americans with many a desperately needed meal, and the eagle has been known to be a seacoast pirate, waiting for the osprey to catch a fish and then robbing the osprey of its meal; it is also a feeder on carrion, like a vulture. Still, in appearance the gobbler is an ungainly, even a comical bird, while the eagle's demeanor is challenging and stately, and its character is far more interesting than Franklin's criticisms indicated.

Courting—in Florida in winter, in the Northeast in early spring, depending on where a given pair may nest —the birds soar above their territory, until the male stoops at his mate, who flips on her back, they lock claws, and then, great wings open, they somersault down together—as Whitman wrote, "a living, fierce, gyrating wheel,/Four beating wings, two beaks, a swirling mass tight grappling . . . ," break apart before they hit the ground or the water, and soar up again, "on slow, firm pinions slanting, their separate diverse flight,/She hers, he his, pursuing."

Faithful to each other for life, the big birds remain faithful to their breeding territory as well, and often build a new nest each season right on top of the last year's nest —the whole construction eventually looking like "a stack of saucers," in the words of Francis H. Herrick, student of the subject. One of these nests, which doubtless had served several generations, is known to have been built up to a height of 20 feet and a width of 10 feet, and nests weighing half a ton, a ton, even two tons, have been recorded.

The construction materials include sticks, cornstalks, weeds, and sod. Though this is usually collected bit by bit, a few eagles have been known to gather their nests in wholesale lots—witness Witmer Stone's story in *Bird Studies at Old Cape May*. Two acquaintances of Stone's were sitting at the edge of a marsh in the spring of 1912, and they saw an eagle stoop at a dome-shaped muskrat house—made of mud and grasses—and come to rest there. "Folding its wings it gazed this way and that and then began to work its feet down into the sods of the house. It gave several flaps with its wings, but with no result, and resumed its foot action. The next effort was more successful and with powerful strokes it arose in the air and with it went the whole top of the muskrats' domicile. As the bird rose higher and higher, showers of dead grass, dirt, and so on, sifted down, but the mass that it took away with it was considerably larger in bulk than its body." Fifteen years later, Stone reported, another New Jersey bald eagle carried off the better part of a small haystack to its nest.

The female lays usually two eggs, rarely three, and if more than one of these hatches, the younger bird or birds are often hard put to survive under the food-hogging, bullying, and downright violent attacks of their elder sibling—the Cain and Abel behavior being characteristic of the young of other large birds of prey as well. In three months, the eaglet grows from a chick three inches long to a fledged, brown bird three feet long, with a wingspan at least six feet and possibly as much as eight and a half feet across. These young birds will remain more or less brown, mottled with white, through the next four years or so, before the head and tail become white, but the chances are very good they will not survive to put on adult plumage; the mortality rates for young bald eagles are very high—shot and natural accident taking large numbers of them. If they have bred or been born in the South, often they fly north during the summer—no one knows why—and return home early in the fall. Northern bald eagles move south later, and some go only far enough to find a reliable source of food—open water with dead fish on the shore and rafts of wintering ducks nearby, a frozen lake on which they may find the carcasses of deer, killed by canine predators.

Bald eagles, not so many years ago, were much more common in the East than they are now. On the Hudson River in late winter or early spring, for instance, it was not unusual to see dozens of them floating downstream, perched on chunks of ice, and at a distance looking, said John Kieran, like lost coal scuttles. One observer saw 25 of them in sight at once on the river. No longer. A population that once bred throughout the Northeast has now shrunk to a handful breeding in the state of Maine, and they have not been doing well there, recently. The competition for space, thrust upon them by man, has doubtless been one cause for the decline, but in the last thirty years, persistent pesticides and their kin are believed to have done considerable damage to eagle reproduction.

The bald eagle that brought us to the lookouts that September morning was probably a Florida bird, so early in the fall, heading home after a summer sojourn on the Northeast coast; it could not offer us any hope for the fate of the bald eagle population breeding—or trying to breed—to the north and east of us. It was an adult; an alarmingly small percentage of bald eagles that have passed the mountain most recent autumns have worn the splotchy brown plumage of young birds, so this bird was nothing to cheer about in that respect either. But few of us see very many eagles in our lifetimes. There are no days at the sanctuary, as there once were, when a dozen or more of these majestic fliers might be seen heading south. So we got out of bed early, hurried to the lookouts, and waited for the mist in the valley to burn off and the air to warm enough for the eagle to soar. When the bird did rise at last, it spiraled back toward the east for a mile or more as it gained altitude, then turned and set and, without a single stroke of its wings, slid down the almost still morning air to pass high over the mountain, between North and South Lookouts. As it disappeared behind the bend in the ridge, someone on North Lookout said, "Godspeed," and the rest of us took it up, like an Amen.

SIX

Sitting at his cluttered desk in Schaumboch's, in what used to be the Brouns' kitchen, an exasperated Alex Nagy is reading aloud from a letter recently published in one of the journals of horticulture. The writer is a professor and a member of the sanctuary association, and he talks about how DDT has clearly not done the damage to wildlife ascribed to it, because at Hawk Mountain—as the member is delighted to note from the annual newsletter—another record high count of ospreys has been made the previous autumn.

"You know," says Alex, waving the journal, "this is the reason we have our doubts about publishing, or even *taking*, a count of hawks in the fall. People like this use our figures—and this guy *knows* you can't use the figures this way."

The rest of us in the office this morning are aware that this has long been a sore point at Hawk Mountain, ever since the pesticides interests began citing the sanctuary's data to show that birds of prey were not being hurt by persistent pesticides. When Maurice Broun started taking the count in 1934, it was because until then no one knew very much about the mechanics and the extent of the hawk migration. The figures served to promote the sanctuary, to bring it members; for one thing, it meant something to be part of an organization that was protecting 15,000 or 20,-000 hawks a year. The members of the association, many of whom helped to take the count, liked to know at the end of every fall just how good a fall it had been and how many hawks had been seen; that remains one of the reasons for taking the count. Over the years, ornithologists have devised ways of using the annual figures to indicate general fluctuations in various species populations and the effects of weather on migration, and a great deal of effort is put into the count-taking in the hope that more and better methods will be designed for interpreting them, but so far it has proven extremely difficult to give the counts any absolute scientific value. There are simply too many variables to take into consideration.

In a nutshell, the count totals in any given year depend on the vagaries of the weather, how many people happen to be involved in taking the count, how expert they are, and where they stand to do their counting.

The human element in the equation defies statistical assessment. Reliable hawk-counting requires sharp vision, alertness, an aptitude for telling different species apart —often at long range and under widely varying weather and light conditions—and a conservative bent that controls one's impulse to give names to hawks that haven't really been seen well enough to identify, and also controls the impulse to count more hawks than are actually in view. Some people are very good at it, others not, and one's expertise does not necessarily bear any relationship to one's enthusiasm for hawks. It's like having a talent for playing the violin. And it requires, above all, practice, hours and hours of sitting on lookouts, watching birds pass.

If you have the knack for identifying birds of prey, then after a while you stop worrying about the field marks the books say you're supposed to look for. "You can tell, just by the *mannerisms* of a bird," said Alex once, "what bird it is. Say a kestrel and a merlin. I don't know if I ever saw a merlin go over the mountain above eye level—hardly ever. They're usually right over the treetops, low. The kestrel is usually a little higher—and it weaves a lot. Little things like that. You see this direct, straight flight, the bird flying low and flapping like anything, well, it's a merlin. You don't even have to go by shape or size or anything. Just by how it's flying you can tell."

I blinked and shook my head. I can't do that yet with most hawks, and I still spend much of my time watching for shape, size, color, and stripes. "It's like—" said Alex, "well, I grew up in the woods with my Dad, you know. He used to take me out and show me all these different trees, and quite often you could look off in the distance and you could tell what the tree was. But it's hard to describe, *why* it's a white oak, or why it's a pin oak. It's the shape, and all that, but then it's a *combination* of things —where it's growing on the hillside, the shape of it, the color of the bark. And hawkwatching is really not different. After you watch so many, your mind becomes a computer. It's just exposure, that's all it is." But ability and exposure vary.

The numbers of hawkwatchers who come to the mountain each day also vary a great deal. One pair of eyes on the lookout is not as good as two, twenty pairs are better than ten, because more sky is being covered at one time. More than that, the presence of company keeps a hawkwatcher on the *qui vive;* everyone likes to be the first to see an approaching bird. The fewer the people on the lookouts, the more birds are likely to be missed.

Counting can be a frantic business for a lone birder. At a spring hawk watch on the southeast corner of Lake Ontario a few years back, a woman arrived early one morning just as the broadwings were beginning to rise from their perches. In a few minutes, there were thousands of birds, circling in five different kettles, and all of them drifting toward her. She had her glasses to her eyes and was desperately tallying hawks, when a New York state trooper pulled up alongside her. "What are you doing?" he demanded.

"Don't ask me any questions now, please," she said, not daring to lower her binoculars. "Just count the birds over there." She waved her hand toward the other end of the swirling phalanx of broadwings. The bemused trooper wanted to know whether he was counting pigeons, or what, but he obliged, and stayed for about an hour. Between them, they counted 5,000 birds.

Under far less pressure than that, it is easy to miss hawks. Anyone who has spent time at it has seen innumerable occasions when although a passing hawk is what is called "a naked-eye bird," sailing close to the lookout, some of the watchers never find it—even when people who see the bird are helpfully giving directions. You can be watching alone, trying to cover all the sky by yourself, and now and then you'll look behind you, just to make sure, and there, by God, is an eagle or a redtail or an osprey—big birds all. How on earth did that get by without being seen, and how many other birds that day have not been seen at all?

Certain kinds of weather make the hawks hard to see: a cloudless blue sky is sheer misery; a few clouds help—by giving relief to the background and providing reference points for the eye; a sky full of clouds is the best. On hot, windless days, the hawks are usually very high and difficult to pick up without using binoculars; but, on the other hand, scanning with binoculars drastically limits the breadth of your view. Some hawks approach the lookouts low, against the background of the trees, which makes missing them easy: peregrines do that; so do merlins and sharpshins and red-shoulders and marsh hawks. The quality of the light makes a difference there, too. If a "good bird" is spotted—an eagle or a goshawk or an osprey —or an interesting group of hawks goes by in a body, chances are everyone will watch it and ignore the possibility that there may be other hawks passing.

Just those day-to-day variables are enough to cast strong doubt on how well the counts represent the actual numbers of migrating birds. In the early years, relatively few people manned the lookouts; now there are more hawk-watchers on the mountain on weekdays than there used to be on some Saturdays and Sundays in the past. Until 1967, the count was taken mainly from one lookout; since then, another major lookout has been opened, and four smaller ones have been used with increasing frequency. This spreading out of the watchers also has added to the hawk totals. So there is simply no good way to compare the counts of the 1940's with the counts of the 1970's.

Then there's the weather. If it happens to be poor throughout a fall, the counts will be low; good, and the counts will be high. The weather can be unhelpful at just the wrong time: the big sharpshin flight usually comes at the end of September and the beginning of October; if the wind blows from the southeast all during that period, the migrating sharpshins will be dispersed over a wide front, and the count will be poor, but if the wind gets into the northwest for two or three days in that period, the sharpies will jam in against the ridge and stream past the lookouts. The difference in the counts can amount to 1,000 or 2,000, maybe more.

And hawks themselves behave in ways that make anyone who is serious about interpreting the counts throw up his hands. With the help of radios, Maurice Broun's research on migrating flight speeds was elaborated on a few years ago. Two volunteers posted themselves at a spot some 13 miles up the ridge; from there, they communicated with the sanctuary whenever an eagle or a peregrine or some distinctive combination of birds went by, and the birds were clocked over that distance. Quite often, even in weather that should have held birds to the ridge, the hawk or hawks in question never showed up over the lookouts. One September afternoon, the two young men radioed that they had thousands of broadwings overhead— "More birds than we can count!" At North Lookout, we waited for this invasion from the east with considerable anticipation, but we saw very few broadwings the rest of the day. The birds went someplace else. Or again, in September 1971, Hawk Mountain saw a record one-day number of ospreys—88; the following day, with a change of wind, only 7 of them were counted. On those same two days, at a hawk watch in New Jersey where the wind held fairly steady, the counts were 13 and 52—the good and the bad osprey days had been reversed. Why? No one knows.

The case of the Hawk Mountain osprey counts, which often sets Alex busily typing letters on his portable electric, is particularly interesting. The eaglelike fish hawks of the Northeast coast went into a terrible decline in the 1950's and 60's. It is estimated that the breeding population on the shore between Boston and New York was down, by 1972, to about one-tenth of what it had been in 1940. As with the collapse of the eastern peregrines, this was the result of a widespread breeding failure, and this failure was carefully documented by observations made in the breeding territories.

The osprey had been a common bird of prey—in terms of visibility, possibly the commonest. It is big, up to two feet long, wings four and a half to six feet across, tip to tip. It nests out in the open, near water, often but not always in colonies. For its nest perch it uses everything from beached crab traps or the sand itself to dead trees and radio towers and the tops of abandoned farmhouses and navigational markers. Ospreys usually build big stick nests on those sites, picking up sticks from the shore or flying at dead tree-limbs to snap them off with their talons. Then they line the nests, and decorate them, with all sorts of objects. One list of osprey construction material, reprinted in

Arthur Cleveland Bent's life history of the species, includes "barrel . . . hoops; bunches of seaweed, long masses of kelp, mullein stalks and cornstalks; . . . parts of oars, a broken boat-hook, tiller of a boat, a small rudder, . . . ; large pieces of fish nets, . . . and pieces of rope, some of them twenty feet in length; . . . a toy boat, with one sail still attached; . . . a small axe with broken handle, . . . a feather duster, a deck swab, a blacking-brush, and a boot-jack; a rubber boot, several old shoes, an old pair of trousers, a straw hat, and part of an oil skin 'sou'wester'; a long fish line, with sinks and hooks attached, wound on a board"—now, *there's* a real fish hawk—"old bottles, tin cans, . . . one rag doll, shells and bright colored stones, a small fruit basket, part of an eel pot, a small worn out door mat. . . ." Also, birds' wings, cattle bones, and sheep skulls. Ospreys mate for life and return to the same nest year after year. Some of these nests, passed on from one generation to the next and added to each spring, become enormous landmarks, drawing the eye. Often one of the birds will be seen perching on the edge of the nest, conspicuous in its size and handsome plumage—dark gray-brown back, white breast, white head with a dramatic black stripe through the eye.

And unlike their mammal-eating cousins, ospreys do their hunting over water, which means—again—out in the open. They row overhead on long, crooked wings, looking down for fish swimming close to the surface, and then pull up, beating wings rapidly while they hover above the prey. They are noisy birds, and as an osprey hovers it may well scream and once more draw attention to itself. Now it stoops, head down, wings up above its back in a sharp V; it thrusts its legs forward parallel to its body, until the talons are in front of the beak. It hits the water and may go completely under after the fish. When it has made a catch, it rises from the water, shaking itself, with the fish almost always already held in the claws—presumably having been caught that way—head foremost, the aerodynamically preferred position; if not, the switch is usually made as the bird gains altitude for the flight to an eating perch or to the nest.

In all things, it is showy. "The Fish-Hawk," wrote Alexander Wilson early in the nineteenth century, "is doubtless the most numerous of all its genus within the United States. It penetrates far into the interior of the country up our large rivers, and their headwaters. It may be said to line the seacoast from Georgia to Canada. In some parts I have counted, at one view, more than twenty of their nests within half a mile." Wilson had not seen the biggest of the known northeastern colonies, on Gardiner's Island at the entrance to Long Island Sound, but he had correspondence with the resident Mr. Gardiner and knew of its size; there were an estimated 300 pairs breeding on the 3,000-acre island every year.

"The first appearance of the Fish-Hawk in spring," Wilson wrote, "is welcomed by the fishermen, as a happy signal of the approach of those vast shoals of herring, shad, &c &c., that regularly arrive on our coasts, and enter our rivers in such prodigious multitudes. Two of a trade, it is said, seldom agree; the adage, however, will not hold good in the present case, for such is the respect paid the Fish-Hawk not only by [fishermen], but generally, by the whole neighborhood where it resides, that a person who should attempt to shoot one of them, would stand a fair chance of being insulted."

The farmers considered it good luck to have an osprey nest near the house. And ospreys did not take chickens; in fact, the farmers believed that ospreys kept away other hawks who might. So they put up old cartwheels or other platforms on the tops of stout poles, as nesting sites to attract the birds.

The numbers of ospreys declined, wherever man's presence grew too obtrusive or did serious damage to the food supply. And where the fishing fell off, some fishermen took to blaming the osprey, not their own overfishing—just as sheep ranchers blame golden eagles for the death of lambs that die because of neglect by both the rancher and the chronically absent-minded ewe; and just as sportsmen blame the goshawk for the scarcity of overshot grouse. The remedy they all chose was the same: shoot the hawk. At least one man also set cruel traps for the osprey: just under the surface of the water, a pitchfork, business-end up and a fish impaled on the tines; the osprey killed itself in its plunge for the fish. And as the ospreys migrated, whether down the shore or along the Applachians, gunners potted at them. But on the whole, the ospreys still did quite well, until their abrupt crash began in the 1950's. The crash reached catastrophic proportions on the Northeast coast by 1970. One colony, at the mouth of the Connecticut River, was estimated by Roger Tory Peterson to have 150 active nests in the 1940's; by 1960, the breeding pairs numbered 72; the next year, 31; in 1965, just 13; in 1971, 3. The famous Gardiner's Island colony collapsed from 200 active nests to 34, just between 1967 and 1971.

The osprey had been, to birders particularly, a favorite hawk—the hawk that didn't hide, a graceful flier, a spectacular fisherman. They watched with dismay the population crash on the coast. Yet at Hawk Mountain, the autumn counts of passing ospreys held quite stable through the 50's and into the 60's—usually around 300 or a little above. In 1963, the count did drop to 190, the lowest since 1940, but the next year it was back to average, and from then on the counts mounted. For the first time in the sanctuary's history, more than 400 ospreys were tallied in 1965. In 1967, the year South Lookout was opened, the record was broken again, and in 1969, the osprey count was over 500. An even 600 were seen in 1970, and 613 the next year. The hawkwatchers were flabbergasted, and many of them became caught up in the spirit of the chase. They *wanted* to set new records.

Tall, lean Fred Wetzel, talented bird artist, protégé of Maurice and Irma Broun, was assistant curator the fall of 1970, and he described the attempt to find the last of the 600 ospreys. "By October 18th . . . the combined osprey count for the season [was] 598. A single bird on the 24th brought the . . . count to 599 and there it remained for the balance of October. Though many sharp-eyed observers remained at the Lookout to the brink of darkness for the remaining days, no additional osprey was anywhere to be seen. . . . November 1st at 2:10 P.M. a large bird was sighted over number one. Sure enough, osprey number 600 was on the way. Its passage was punctuated by a spontaneous cheer from all observers present."

The persevering hawkwatchers have added considerably to the osprey counts by staying on the lookouts evening after evening, much later than they might have otherwise, specifically to count ospreys. After four or five in the afternoon, the hawk flight thins to almost nothing, even on good days. The die-hards may see an occasional eagle or goshawk or—most likely—osprey, sailing past, low, on the fading wind and heat. But ordinarily, few watchers would put off attending to their own creature comforts, a soft place to sit, a bath, a drink, and some supper, just for the sake of those few scattered birds, particularly after a day full of hawks. To be sure, Maurice and Alex used to stay late on the Observation Rocks some evenings to count eagles and ospreys; and the spacious solitude of the mountaintop at day's end now and then holds a few watchers there long after everyone else has left. But such regular and numerous late-staying, to build up the count, was a new phenomenon, and it did have its effect. On the 88-osprey day in 1971, for example, 30 of the birds were counted after five o'clock.

The number of lookouts also added to the osprey totals. But even making allowances for all these factors, the crash of the coastal ospreys was certainly not reflected by the sanctuary's counts. The boosters of persistent pesticides seized on the counts as proof that somehow all the observations from the coast were wrong, that in fact the osprey was increasing at an amazing rate.

Alex tends to treat the records gingerly. He believes that the many variables involved in the counts make it impossible for anyone to interpret them with assurance—period. However, some defensible use has been made of the counts by others, who tried, for example, lumping together the figures of several successive years for one species or another, and comparing these totals with the totals for other clusters of years. And the president of the Hawk Mountain Sanctuary Association, Joseph Taylor (a peripatetic birder who has seen more different species of North American birds than any other man alive), has suggested an explanation for the recent osprey totals that assumes more ospreys are indeed passing Hawk Mountain than did a few years ago. If his explanation proved to be as accurate as it is plausible, it would simply reinforce the evidence of the coastal collapse.

To begin with, no one knows just where Hawk Mountain's hawks are coming from. In this regard the ospreys are no exception. It stands to reason they're not coming from the coast, because if they were they would have to fly inland for some distance until they reached the Appalachian chain. Ospreys are seen migrating down the coast in the fall, and in all probability that's the route followed by coastal breeding ospreys, as well as by some inland breeders that fly south along the river valleys until they reach salt water. Hawk Mountain's ospreys would then have to be coming from someplace else. There is a population breeding on fresh-water lakes, far from the sea. Very little is known about them—how many they are and where, exactly, they nest. But Joseph Taylor thinks it possible that those make up the bulk of Hawk Mountain's ospreys, and that as the coastal colonies were being decimated, the inland breeders found less and less competition on the wintering grounds, hence more of them survived the winters, and the population increased. It's an interesting idea. The lack of information on these inland breeders could indicate that they don't exist in great numbers, or that they nest in regions—say, in northern Maine, New Brunswick, Newfoundland, the interior of northern Quebec—too remote and trackless for peregrinating birders to get to, unless they made a project of it.

Just such a project has been discussed at Hawk Mountain for several years. Alex would like to organize teams of hardy hawkwatchers to explore various sample areas from which the ospreys might be coming—on the coast as well as inland. Once a team found nests, it would wait until just before the young birds were ready to fly, then climb to the nests and color-dye the birds, a different color for each sample area. Color-dying has already been used to help ornithologists track migrating gulls. The hawkwatchers would then, literally, sit back and wait—not just at Hawk Mountain, but along the shore and at various other hawk watches on the Appalachian chain—and records of the sightings of dyed ospreys would give the migration researchers some idea of which migrants originate where and what routes they follow south, and when.

However, this is an enormous undertaking. The field teams would have to be recruited, organized, instructed, and probably to some extent outfitted. The birders of the Northeast would have to be alerted to the project and some sort of dependable watching network assured for the fall, in the face of the limitations imposed on hawkwatchers by their jobs, families, and household chores. So far, the sanctuary has had neither the time nor the money to begin the project. For that matter, although it has functioned informally as a clearing house for data from a loose collection of hawk watches in the Northeast, it has just not had the manpower to oversee the kind of eastern hawkwatching organization that it would like to have developed long before this, to multiply the possibilities for research on migration patterns. The material is there; Hawk Mountain has spawned many a birder's passion for hawkwatching, and these alumni, so to speak, have found their own lookouts elsewhere, new ones every year. But, as usual, there is more than enough work for the sanctuary staff to do, year round, without adding any new duties.

Here is Alex at his desk—two desks, really, side by side, piled with magazines and professional journals and bulging file folders and the unending correspondence. Bridging a couple of the stacks of magazines is a slab of stained wood that he evidently plans to turn into one of his innumerable signs—handsomely carved and decorated with his paintings, mostly of hawks—that help visitors find their way in the sanctuary and, as one of Alex's gestures of community goodwill, around nearby villages as well. On the desk in front of him, on top of a dozen letters awaiting attention, and half-hidden by the journal open to the offending osprey-count letter, is a map of the lower reaches of the sanctuary. The sanctuary has grown from its original 1,400 to 2,100 acres, and now includes the River of Rocks and beyond, and much of that eastern end of the property in the Kettle, along Kettle Creek, is ecologically different from the flanks and tops of the ridge. Alex and Jim Brett have been discussing a plan for a trail that will branch off from one now winding through the River of Rocks and bend down along the creek to meet the Appalachian Trail, which crosses through the end of the property near Eckville. The territory down there is crisscrossed by dozens of old logging roads, so what is needed is the choice of a scenic route and trail markings to keep the visitor from getting lost.

Dick Sharadin, assistant curator, listens to us talk about counting ospreys and quietly adds a word of his own here and there, as he completes a fair copy of yesterday's hour-by-hour, species-by-species count records. The sanctuary is trying to increase the scientific value of the counts, so those records include columns for separating the birds by age and sex, when possible; other migrating birds besides hawks also are noted on the tally sheets. When Dick is done with that, he will pull out a set of blank tally sheets, unplug one of the walkie-talkies, which have been charging all night, and go up to South Lookout to take the day's count with whoever joins him. One of the volunteers will be in charge at North Lookout, and a few of us will be at Owl's Head.

Compact, dark-haired, gentle, Dick began as a member of the association and now has Alex's old job. Out of the hawking season, he builds the walls, does the planting, repairs buildings, takes charge of whatever young volunteers are on hand to help out. In the autumn, he is on the lookouts most weekdays and some weekend days—when he is not taking admissions and selling books at the entrance. He is one of the best field birders, when it comes to hawks, in the East.

In the far corner, facing Alex across a couple of shoved-together tables, his view hemmed in by the file cabinets in the middle of the room, Jim Brett copes with some of his correspondence while he waits for the day's first busload of children. He will lead three of those onto the trails today; a local Scout troop will also be here, but Jim has arranged for the leaders to use the cassette lecture. There hasn't been a noticeable gap in the parade of these groups since February. In the old days, Alex says, there were few student visitors around in the summer. "But now they have these summer enrichment programs. When I went to school, vacation was vacation—free and easy. Now they go back to school again in the summertime. So we don't have a real break except in the dead of winter."

And winter provides no break in the other work. December is the deer-hunting season, when everybody is out patrolling the bounds all day. The state has 6,000 acres of game lands adjoining the sanctuary, and when the season starts, the deer flee to the protection of Hawk Mountain; for some hunters, the temptation to chase them across the boundary is overwhelming. January and February are the months when, between expeditions to repair storm damage in the sanctuary, the newsletter is readied for the printer, and the membership, reminded about annual dues; when the Hawk Mountain slide show, which is almost constantly in the mail, shuttling between the sanctuary and schools and bird clubs, may be reviewed and revised; when the battle over what should be done about the gypsy moth heats up again—sometimes with the state, more often with the local people who want the sanctuary to spray the mountain. (The last such spraying by the state, which was carried out despite the sanctuary's vigorous objection, killed off all the honeybees on the mountain, and they did not begin to recover for three years, while the gypsy moths were back in force almost immediately.) January and February can also be starving months for the deer. Alex and Dick Sharadin keep tabs on them, and when necessary, fodder is cut and put out for them, sometimes with the help of local Boy Scouts. Without predators to keep the deer in check, they overpopulate the sanctuary, and once in a while Hawk Mountain even has to permit a few hunters to come in and thin the herd, to give the survivors a better chance.

The visitors are comparatively few those months; the road over the mountain can become almost as frightful as it was when Maurice and Irma Broun first arrived. But when it is clear, there are always a few people dropping into Schaumboch's, coming through the door into what was once the Broun's living room and is now a reception room, with a big oval hooked rug on the wide-boarded floor, a few chairs and tables standing around the perimeter, one wall lined with nature books for sale, and here and there —leaning, stacked, or hung—paintings by members of the sanctuary, usually also for sale. Barbara Lake, the cheery secretary, has her desk in there and acts as a buffer between the office and potential interruptions. But then, as on this day in October, the regulars filter into the low-beamed office anyway, to chat, and new visitors, peering through the door and seeing all the activity, step in behind them. To find six or eight people there at a time is not unusual. Alex is proud of the personal touch at Hawk Mountain and enjoys it himself, but I am sure that he hopes we will all clear out for the lookouts pretty quick and leave him some space and quiet so he can get at his paperwork.

Despite the interruptions—for that matter, despite the fact that getting up to the lookouts for hawkwatching has become a luxury he can allow himself very seldom—it is a privilege to live on the mountain as Alex does. Each January, for the annual newsletter, he writes a month-by-month record of the past year up to the fall, at which point he gives way to assistant curator Dick Sharadin's report of the fall hawking season. Alex's enjoyment of what he does is obvious. He writes, for example, of the sanctuary in February: "White-tailed deer, tho more numerous in the lowlands, do spend some time 'pawing' out the acorns which have collected in the gullies; several oval-compressed patches reveal their bedding areas. Curiously their superb insulating hairs are so well developed . . . as not to melt the snow they were lying on. . . . Tiny, crisscrossed, paired tracks with tail prints are evidence of the white-footed mouse, occasionally disappearing in a hole in the snow, only to reappear a short distance later. The large hole punched into a snow bank may be a mystery, but not to the grouse that spent last night there. Meandering fox tracks are exciting. We find mostly grays, but reds are increasing as the forest matures. The red fox's prints are larger and longer, also the fur between the toes often obscures the toenails. The gray's are much smaller and more roundish, much like a cat, but with the toenails showing."

So Alex tracks through the seasons, following the life of the mountain—the grouse and the wild turkey and the pileated woodpeckers and the deer and the chestnut oaks and the dogwood and the millions of small plants and the moths and the Allegheny red ants that build their hills three feet high in the middle of small clearings they make themselves by killing the encroaching saplings.

After many years' absence, bobcats are back on the mountain. They were once extirpated by shot. There is less danger of that happening again than there was, particularly if they stay within the bounds of the sanctuary; by state law, it now costs a hunter $50 if he shoots a bobcat and gets caught. That might not deter some men from shooting, if they knew what a bobcat looked like. One hunter reported seeing "the funniest dog" just off the sanctuary, Alex said with a grin. "It had run by, he said. It looked like a small collie with long legs and a very short tail." Alex laughed as he told the story. "I said maybe somebody shot the tail off. 'Yeah,' he said, 'that's exactly what it looked like. Looked like the tail was shot off.' I'm sure he saw the bobcat. So I said, 'What kind of footprint did it have?' 'Oh,' he said, 'big, round footprints, maybe two, two-and-a-half inches in diameter.'" That, indeed, would have been some collie.

One night, about eleven o'clock, Alex stepped out onto the terrace of the curator's house: "I heard the awfullest screaming going on. There was the bobcat; it sounded like it was between here and the South Lookout. Really, it's a strange kind of call. It reminds you of a loud house cat, a screaming cat; you know, if you step on a cat's tail, how it screams? Well, something like that, but deeper, more guttural."

In spring, the geese pass over the mountain by the thousands; warblers and other small birds flock through on southwesterly winds—sometimes few, sometimes many, depending on the weather and how the birds did the previous nesting season and how bad the winter was. Alex used to spend warm spring nights out on the Pinnacle, where sometimes all night he could hear the chips of these small birds flocking north, and in the morning the trees might be swarming with them as they came down to feed and rest. Hawks, too, sail by in the spring, but the lay of the land does not concentrate the northward hawk flight at the mountain the way it does when they are headed south.

Summers, there are thousands of nesting birds on the mountain, hummingbirds sipping at their feeders on the back porch of Schaumboch's, a profusion of flowers, of insects, each year somewhat different than the last, as if one added new books to a much used, much loved collection. Autumns—the hawks, geese headed south, and calling overhead, sometimes all night and all day, loons trading to and from the Great Lakes, the warblers and the thrushes and the finches browsing their way down the Kittatinny, away from frost and failing food supplies in the Northeast. Winters—the birds at the feeders, the tracks in the snow.

The lookout at Owl's Head is merely a narrow shelf, 10 feet long and not much more than a yard across, at the edge of a precipitous slide of boulders. One gets to it from above, down a steep and narrow path that has been skidded out by hawkwatchers trying to avoid picking up speed and pitching off into space. Encumbered often by a pack, a walkie-talkie, and a telescope, one keeps at least a hand free to snatch at passing trees and rocks for handholds. Once on the ledge, the watcher may feel most comfortable behind the waist-high boulder that closes in one end of the lookout. I do. Or you can sit in the open, with feet dangling.

The great slanting cove between Owl's Head and Pinnacle lies below, the rockslide leading down from our perch to the trees that bank the sides of the cove and much of its bottom. To the left, where the cove empties into the Kettle, there are a few pastures, cornfields, the Nagy farm (among others), a parking lot for the hunters using the state game lands, the village of Eckville. An Indian trail used to pass down that way; it probably followed about the same route over the mountain that the state highway does now. Many early settlers were killed near the trail, and doubtless more than a few Indians. Beyond Eckville rises the Donat. Someplace beneath us, to our left, the Appalachian Trail crosses the road, winds away through the woods across the Kettle and up the side of the ridge's main stem, where it meets a side trail called Skyline. That trail follows the top of the ridge to North Lookout. It is a rough hike in places, all ups and downs over huge boulders. It was along the worst of that trail that the phone line was laid for the first flight-speed studies. At one point, where the Hawk Mountain boundary crosses the trail, there's a weathered sign marking the sanctuary; the sign is so worn, it must have been posted many years ago by Maurice Broun.

This is a marsh hawk day, at least at Owl's Head. I never see one of these lovely birds drifting by—long, narrow wings tilted up, white rump showing at the base of the long, narrow tail—that I don't think of quiet salt marshes, particularly in sunset, with marsh hawks hunting low over the edges and the creeks, the pale gray and white bodies of the males, the chocolate brown bodies of the females and young birds washed crimson by the low sun.

One such evening, as I walked a path beside a bay, a marsh hawk a hundred yards away stooped for something in the grass, rose 10 feet or so, dropped whatever it had in its claws, stooped again to snatch it, rose again, dropped its catch. I finally put my glasses on it, to find that it was stooping at a stick, playing with it, practicing idly—like a small boy throwing a tennis ball against a fence to practice fielding grounders.

One observer in the 30's wrote of seeing a marsh hawk do the same thing with a horned lark, a small, sparrow-sized bird—play with it exactly as a cat does with a mouse. "When the lark [having been caught and dropped] reached the ground," he wrote, "the hawk lit beside it, then gave a little jump into the air and landed with spread talons upon its prey. It seemed not to bite the lark, but after examining it with many twistings and turnings of the head rose about three feet into the air with it, and then dropped it again, the lark still fluttering, and pounced upon it as before. This the marsh hawk did seven or eight times. . . . At length the lark fluttered into a tangle of shrubby weeds, which circumstance seemed to furnish even more interest for the hawk. It would prance about in the weeds, taking great high steps, and now and again bend down to peer intently at the lark." The birder lost sight of the action after a while and did not see the denouement.

The marsh hawk is a particularly buoyant flier, having very long wings in relation to its size and weight. In spring, on its breeding territory, the pale gray male can be a marvelous acrobat, exhibiting for a potential mate—or mates; according to recent observations, it is sometimes something of a bigamist, and even a trigamist. It towers up hundreds of feet, and then noses over, somersaults, dives, somersaults again, dives, somersaults, looping downward over and over that way until it is about to hit the ground, and then pulls out and rings up again. Or it may roller-coaster along, in a series of short swoops, at the top of each swoop stalling, sometimes somersaulting, before it drops into the next.

Most often, however, one sees it hunting. Its head is shaped something like an owl's, and more than other hawks it is constructed to look downward as it flies. Its face is built rather like a feather-fringed parabolic reflector, with eyes and beak in the middle; the reflector soaks up and concentrates the sounds of prey. The marsh hawk quarters its hunting territory, tacking first in one direction, then another, then back, a pattern that has given it its other name, "harrier" (after the hare-hounds—harriers—that hunt rabbits in the same zigzagging way). It stays usually no more than 20 or 30 feet off the ground, flapping half a dozen times, then sailing—body rocking slightly beneath the wings—and flapping again. When the female is on the nest, brooding eggs or chicks, and the hunting male returns with food, she flaps up from the ground and in mid-air takes the food from him—either rolling on her back to receive it claw to claw, or flipping sideways to catch it as he drops it.

Marsh hawks have eclectic tastes in food. They don't nest only in salt marshes; they can be found in wet meadows and open prairie, and wherever they may be, they will feed on what prey is available, including mice, voles, squirrels, rabbits, gophers, frogs, snakes, insects, chickens, ducks, grouse, shore birds, songbirds. It is, however, basically a mouser, though that reputation does not impress some hunters even now. One former Hawk Mountain gunner still shoots marsh hawks, and calls them "real killers," because among the prey they really kill are game birds—the hunter's pets, to be sure.

A discovery by the Bureau of Biological Survey in the 1920's is instructive in this regard. There were 30 marsh hawks roosting in a bobwhite preserve in the South. As a reflex action, about half of the hawks were shot before someone thought to check to see just how much damage they were actually doing to the quail. Like owls, hawks swallow a lot of fur and bone with their meat and then regurgitate the indigestible material in pellets or "castings"; examining the pellets found in the marsh hawk roost revealed the remains of four bobwhites, while in more than nine hundred pellets were the bones of an important enemy of the quail, the cotten rat.

In any kind of weather, even on winds that hold most other hawks to the main stem of the ridge, the light-bodied marsh hawks often break away and turn south before they reach North Lookout. Since South Lookout was opened and this perch at Owl's Head began to be manned fairly often, the sanctuary's annual counts of marsh hawks have almost doubled. Today we see dozens of them. All but a few are passing at eye level or below, and are headed up the center of the cove to rise over the back of the Pinnacle spur and drop down to the south side of the ridge. We get used to looking for them at that altitude, but every now and then we scan upward, and far overhead—perhaps a mile high—a speck has appeared that turns out, in the binoculars, to be a harrier, set and gliding southwest. Well, they all count; but as I make the mark on my tally sheet under Marsh Hawk, I wonder how many more of them have got by us up there, and how many are actually too high to be seen.

GOLDEN EAGLE

SEVEN

The air was bright as spring water this November morning when I woke. Through the kitchen window of his parents' house in Minersville, Frank Haas and I could see clouds sailing out of the northwest, and we rushed through our breakfast and the making of sandwiches for lunch, so as to get up on the mountain before the hawks started flying. But when we cleared the woods above North

Lookout, though it was just eight o'clock, the redtails were already strung out along the ridge, obviously in a hurry to get going.

These are the days I live for—frost on the grass and on the rattling cornstalks, wind whipping against the flanks of the ridge, trees bending, and above the tossing bronze and purple landscape, clouds racing toward the sea, hawks streaking southwest. November is the month of the most powerful-looking birds of prey—redtails, rough-legs, golden eagles, and goshawks—fit reflections all of the bright, blustery, heavy-clouded, treacherous weather.

First the redtails this morning, headed south from breeding territory in—at a guess—Quebec, Newfoundland, and Maine, places of too much cold and too little available food in winter. Redtails are known to remain as far north as northern New England in winter; a pair may move some distance from the breeding territory, or stay nearby but change the boundaries of the area in which they hunt. But their offspring and some of the other breeding-age redtails move south because the land will only support so many of them.

There is a good mix of ages going by this morning. Adults with brown backs and broad, russet tails; from underneath they are more or less pale, with brown streaking that thickens into a distinctive band across the belly. The birds born this year are not red-tailed yet; their tails are brown with thin, black stripes. They are mottled brown on their backs and usually somewhat darker than older redtails. But there is great variety in redtail plumages: one western race can be very dark all over, and another can be very light; in the East, such divergencies are not so marked, but there is heavy barring on the bellies of some and almost none on others.

We are getting close looks at them, because the wind is holding them against the ridge. This is a lot closer than most of us normally see redtails. On territory, they are easily spooked, and whether hunting or resting, they often perch on a high branch of a bare tree out in the middle of a meadow. That makes them relatively easy to find if you're looking for them, but it also makes it impossible for a birder to approach one of them without being seen. A man on foot crossing the meadow will scare a redtail off its perch when the distance between them is still as great as a quarter of a mile or more. He could approach closer by car, or on horseback, but once he gets out or dismounts, that's it; the hawk leaves. Even when soaring overhead, prospecting for a meal, the redtail usually keeps its distance. Perhaps the species has developed a genetic distrust of man and awareness of how far shot will carry.

All the soaring Buteos, but particularly the redtails, with their four-foot wingspans, are the farmer's chicken hawks. They often nest in farming areas; pastureland and cornfields are home to many a mouse. Because they do soar out in the open, they can be conspicuous to a man keeping an eye peeled for what might be after his chickens. From time to time, an individual redtail, particularly a young or a sick one, will take a pullet, and a few may make it a regular habit if the pickings are good, but most redtails shot for chicken-thieves will turn out to have nothing in their crops but mice.

Hunting, the redtail may perch in a bare tree above a likely spot and wait for a mouse or a rabbit or a snake to show itself. At times, it circles high up above its territory, and once aloft, it frequently behaves in a way that makes it identifiable at very long range—holding an "aerial perch" for long stretches of time. Arthur Cleveland Bent described it: "Once, as I stood on the brink of a precipice looking down over a broad valley, I saw below me a red-tailed hawk floating over the valley and looking downward for game; it was facing a strong wind and was perhaps buoyed up by rising air currents, as it was poised as motionless as if suspended on a wire; it remained in one spot for three or four minutes and then sailed to another spot a few rods away, where it hung for a similar period."

Once the redtail spots its quarry from the air, it goes into a stoop, and though the dive may be steep and end directly with a kill at the bottom, the hawk is likely to hyphenate the attack at least once—landing first on the exposed branch of a tree near the prey, perhaps waiting a bit to be sure of its aim, then casting off in a shallow dive to make the capture. It is said that if the prey is a big snake, the hawk will land on the ground nearby and perform a threatening dance, with its wings out, encouraging the snake to strike, and strike, and strike again, until the snake is exhausted and vulnerable.

Here on the mountain we often see passing redtails whose normally sleek appearance is distorted by swollen throats, bulges like goiters—a full crop, a recent meal. "You know what's amazing about that?" says Alex. "You can go all day long and you may not see distended crops, and all of a sudden almost every hawk that comes through, the crop is distended. Now, what's the stimulation to feed all of a sudden? I've seen it happen many, many times." Occasionally, an osprey will pass with a fish in its talons; or one of the falcons may appear carrying prey, and bend its head to take a bite as it flies by.

The hawks' need for food on migration was used by some hunters in the past to bring the birds within range. A pigeon, often blinded or crippled, was tied by string to the end of a long pole, and as the hawk approached, the pole was waved, the pigeon fluttered its wings, and the hawk —seeing a potential meal that was obviously not in condition to escape easily—swerved to attack. Something of the sort is still done to trap redtails—and other hawks —so that they may be banded; and falconers often use similar methods to capture their sporting birds. But on migration, most of the redtails that are lured to capture in this way are the inexperienced birds of the year. The adults have learned caution, and when they get close enough to see all the nets and the ropes and the trussed-up pigeon, they veer off. In fact, the young of any of the birds of prey on their first migration are in much greater danger of all kinds than their parents. Their mortality rates, based on bird-band returns, are extremely high. Leslie Brown and Dean Amadon, in a thoroughgoing modern work on predatory birds, report that of 361 redtails whose bands were returned, 265 had been taken from birds that died in the first year of life. People deliver a good many wounded and dead birds to Hawk Mountain—the wounded birds to be cured, the dead birds to be used some way for study or exhibits—and Alex estimates that there are 15 or 20 immature redtails brought in for every adult. The young can get into all sorts of trouble—not just being shot, but breaking a leg or a wing at the bottom of a stoop, or tangling with prey too strong for it, or starving because of inexpertise, or getting sick after not seeking good shelter in a storm. The possibilities are many, and only the smart and the lucky survive.

All day, although the wind is blowing out of the northwest, the weather moves at us from the west—crowds of thick, gray clouds that draw shadows beneath them across

Broad and Sharp and Second mountains, across the wide valley, then sweep overhead and drop rain on us, and pass on, drawing sunlight behind, and behind the sunlight, other ranks of clouds. It is worth being on the mountaintop just for the weather.

Mostly between showers, the hawks sail by. In midmorning, the redtails pass at the rate of more than one a minute—no great concentration, but an ample reward for our puttings on and takings off of rain gear. In the hour between ten and eleven, we count 72 redtails, a goshawk, a Cooper's, a sharpshin, and the sanctuary's rarest regular visitor, a rough-legged hawk.

This is only the sixth roughleg of the season. Some years, none at all get this far south. Like the osprey, the peregrine, the marsh hawk, and the golden eagle, the roughleg breeds in an area that extends well beyond North America. It nests mainly in the Arctic tundra—Siberia, Scandinavia, Alaska, Canada—and the reach of its southward migrations depends on the supply of food in the north. In years when the lemmings' population explodes, so does the roughlegs', and the adults and young stay on the breeding territory longer than usual. When they move south those winters, they do not travel very great distances. But in the lean years when the lemming population collapses, the roughlegs move south ahead of the snow, sometimes in large groups, rather like the broadwings. They make for territory where mice and the like are plentiful. In the Northeast, most roughlegs winter on salt marshes and beaches. One recognizes them, too, a long way off by the way they often hunt, for the roughleg— biggest of the North American Buteos—is the only member of the Buteo family regularly to hold an aerial perch in the manner of the smallest of the North American falcons, the kestrel—by beating its wings. It hovers, so, over a patch of marsh, usually quite low, head cocked for prey, then drifts off with a flap or two and a glide, to pull up again, wings beating.

Considerable numbers of roughlegs used to be seen inland in the Northeast, as well as on the coast, but farmers and sportsmen simply shot out that part of the population. One Massachusetts gentleman—whether for fun or for science, it is impossible to tell—shot hundreds of them in the Connecticut River valley in his lifetime, during the last century; he reported to Dr. A. K. Fisher that he had examined many stomachs of roughlegs and could testify he had never found anything there but mice. One wonders why, once he had begun to get the picture, he kept shooting. Charley Thomas, the Hamburg gunner, says that when he was shooting hawks on the mountain the roughlegs were far more common than they are now. Whatever the reason may be, in no year since Maurice Broun came to the mountain in 1934 have more than three dozen of these big Buteos been counted here.

They are handsome birds. As with the redtails, there are variations in plumage. In the Northeast, there is the light phase, usually with black belly and black-striped breast when seen from below, heavy black patches at the wrists and black edging around the borders of the great, broad, pale wings; and the dark phase, with breast and belly all soot black, the black wrist patches expanded inward in a triangle whose base joins the black of the body. Heavy, regal block-prints of hawks.

In the middle of the day, a marsh hawk passes, and that reminds me of my story about the harrier practicing with its stick. The watchers get to talking about the playfulness of hawks. Frequently, as birds pass the mountain, they are engaged in games with their companions in migration; they dive at each other, sideslip to escape, arc up in brief beak-to-tail dogfights, then separate and fly on. One can see the same sort of play around a nest late in the summer—for example, the parent hawks and their young, or just the young birds, may be spiraling up together, and then one bird breaks off and nonchalantly rises away, turns once it has gained altitude over one of its fellows, and folds its wings for a stoop, which it breaks off just before it would strike. The hawk that served as target may turn on its back at that instant; the two birds come together and bounce apart, without touching—the speed of the action set off by the lazy slide that separates them afterward. Then they come together again, twisting, flipping to-one-side-then-the-other, pulling up, diving, braking, and planing easily away as if innocent of any teasing intent, very much like children in a prolonged game of tag pretending (who, *me?*) that now the game is over and waiting for the other to relax his guard. I once watched five kestrels in just such a game, above a high cliff. Every now and then, a group of crows would join in. A kestrel would attack one of its own, then peel off and dive on a crow; the crow would dodge, flap to gain altitude, and dive in its turn. One or two of the kestrels would break off and soar out over the edge of the cliff and wait on there in the air—resting, perhaps—until another kestrel or a crow passed within range. The crows grew tired of the sport after 15 minutes or so, but the dashing little falcons were still at it a half hour after they began.

The game would not likely get serious. And most of these combats we see as the hawks pass the mountain appear harmlessly meant and harmlessly taken. But there are certain elements of bullying and braggadocio in even a playful attack, and Maurice Broun once watched an overly cocky red-shoulder, harassing a golden eagle a mile and a half high over Hawk Mountain, suddenly become a meal for the eagle, which rolled on its back, snatched the red-shoulder, and dived to the woods below to eat.

There are life-and-death overtones in all such play. This is practice, exercise, a source of experience. The hawk that knows which birds are stronger and should be avoided, the hawk that is faster than its fellows, more agile in flight, more dextrous with its talons, more courageous, more confident, that hawk will survive longest.

Do hawks *know* this? Sometimes, as with my marsh hawk, they play all by themselves. I remember a Hawk Mountain story about such play, with one small detail that enlarges the event so greatly for me I feel as if I'd been given a quick look through a door opening on immeasurable, unknowable wildness. It was a simple enough situation. An immature redtail drifted slowly past North Lookout, well out over the valley, on a gray afternoon when the wind was streaming out of the northwest and blowing leaves across the view. The hawk was fascinated by the possibilities presented by the leaves. It spiraled up, stooped, struck at a flying leaf, crushed and dropped it; spiraled up, dived, struck at another leaf, crushed and dropped it; spiraled up, stooped, struck at a monarch butterfly, crushed and dropped it, spiraled up . . .

At the north edge of the lookout, the dead stem of a sapling, 15 feet tall, has been jammed upright into a hole between rocks. On its top sits a papier-mâché owl, slightly on the tilt, with a few white paper strips tied beneath its feet and fluttering—supposedly the feathers of a victim. The owl has been raised there today, as it often is, for another sort of game, in the hope it will bring a few hawks in close. Owls and hawks are not friendly toward each other, and the little sharpshins, particularly, take umbrage at the presence of even an askew owl decoy and will make considerable detours to harass it. Now and then they actually swipe at its head—which does no damage to our friend of cardboard except to scar the top of its head a bit; but some years ago, one watcher brought up a stuffed great horned owl, and when he took the owl back down the mountain that day, it was without a head, thanks to a bold sharpie.

We try to encourage the attack as birds approach by blowing on wooden predator calls, which presumably make a noise like wounded prey. A former assistant curator here used to be able to whistle them in occasionally, without such aids. One weekend afternoon, he said, he was on the lookout and chatting about this talent, and a lady with a box camera overheard him. She made her way over boulders until she was beside the pole, aimed her camera up at the owl decoy, and waited. A sharpshin appeared high overhead. "Call it down," the lady asked him. He knew that was ridiculous; he hadn't intended to give the impression that his whistling, however talented, worked on more than one sharpshin in five hundred. But he lifted his head and whistled, and the sharpie dropped like a stone toward the owl, braking about a foot above it. For an instant, the hawk was suspended there, motionless; the lady clicked her camera, thanked the assistant curator cordially, and clambered back across the lookout, obviously convinced it happened all the time.

For the fourth time today, gray clouds have blown over us, the rain has begun to fall, and we have put on ponchos and slickers. Occasionally, a hawk disdains to sit down and wait out the shower, as it ought, and slides past us, close to the lookout. But as soon as we pull out binoculars, the optics are covered with rain and condensation that muddies our view. Handkerchiefs are soon too wet to be much use drying the glasses, and here, stroking powerfully toward us, comes a large, dark bird—too big and too dark to be anything but a golden eagle. All day, each time the wind gusted up, Frank has been saying "Eagle wind!" as usual, and we have hoped he was right. So here it is, as close as one could want. But the light is too poor, and the eagle possibly too wet, for the feathers of the head and neck and shoulders to shine golden as they should, and all that our binoculars show us, as rain streams down our faces, is a dark shape and fog on the lenses. The eagle drives past and is gone, something of an anticlimax.

Well, there will be others. Hawk Mountain and vicinity is becoming a fairly reliable place to see golden eagles even in the middle of winter, and there have also been a few recent records of summering eagles—birds either past their prime, apparently, or not yet old enough to breed. One June day a few years ago, for example, Alex happened to notice, from his car, a troop of crows harassing a vulture. There was something wrong with that picture, and a mile or so farther on he remembered what it was: crows wouldn't be pestering a vulture in June. He swung the car around and went back to look. The "vulture" was a male golden eagle, an individual so old that its hackles had turned from gold to gray. It was not much of a hunter any longer. Alex's father used to see it beating back and forth over his farm, and, occasionally, it tried to hunt there. One day, it was after ring-necked pheasants feeding in a cornfield. "The eagle would come down," Alex says, "and he'd fly between the corn rows—he'd fold his wings—

trying to drive these pheasants out into the open. And after he did drive a couple out, he'd stoop at them and he'd miss, and he'd go up again, and stoop at them, and miss." His father said afterward he felt so sorry for the eagle he had considered getting a shotgun and shooting one of the pheasants for him.

The elder Nagy was also raising sheep at the time, and hunger made the eagle brave enough to make a pass at one of the lambs, while the farmer looked on. No damage was done. When the eagle stooped, the ewe nickered softly, her two lambs hustled in under her belly, and the eagle soared away. The same thing happened again, and finally the eagle landed on the ground near the ewe, presumably to figure out a better method of attack, and with the two lambs still hugging to her she walked up to the eagle, stared at him mildly, and turned and walked away.

Much of the time, the old eagle was reduced to eating carrion like a vulture, particularly road kills—which doubtless gave a number of motorists something of a start. The first time Alex's wife Arlene saw the eagle, it was blocking her way down the state road, its three-foot wings spread threateningly in defense of its meal.

A sad comedown. The golden eagle in its prime is a chaser after flying grouse and racing hares, a sharp-eyed hunter circling high above a prairie-dog town, cannily waiting for the dogs to forget it is there, a bird of enormous strength and courage, willing and capable of taking on prey much bigger than itself. The Tartars and Mongols as they have for centuries still train golden eagles to hunt wolves, which the eagles cannot lift but are strong enough to incapacitate or kill. On big game, the eagles may hunt in teams; in his book on the golden eagle, Seton Gordon quotes a head stalker on a Scottish deer preserve: "I had just stalked and shot a stag out of a small mixed lot of stags and hinds, and was keeping the herd under observation with a view to getting another stag later on, when an eagle stooped on and struck a calf a terrific blow with her body. As far as I could see the eagle did not attempt to fix her talons or bill in the calf; she simply swooped down at a terrific pace, her wings folded and legs up close to her body. Scarcely had she ascended when another eagle attacked in the same manner, and then a third. All three birds adopted the same method of attack . . . the calf was pretty well grown, and avoided a good many blows by wheeling sharply in little circles just as one of the big birds approached; but attack followed attack so quickly that he very soon got exhausted, and then one of the eagles fixed her talons in his withers and, flapping her huge wings savagely, bore the calf to the ground."

They have been seen, working in pairs, to cut an animal out of a herd of deer or antelope, steer the prey toward a precipice by flying at it and sometimes beating it with their wings, and, ultimately, drive it over the cliff to be killed on the rocks below, and then eaten. They are known to kill full-grown antelope, singly or in teams, in another fashion: they land on the animal's back, and while it leaps and bucks, trying to shake off the eagle, the talons grip the spine, the eagle hammers with its beak at the region of the backbone. Eventually, the animal collapses, either from exhaustion and terror or from a spinal injury.

When we see migrating eagles here, they are just loafing along. Their loose-jointed flapping of those big wings reminds me of a first-rate athlete casually jogging onto a field. But it is a bird of such power and accuracy in the air that a pair can overtake a fleeing grouse without so much as stirring a wing except to steer; the lead bird can knock down the grouse and not grapple it, and the following eagle will snatch the stunned prey as it falls.

All this was beyond the old eagle that frequented Nagy's farm. It had not lost its canniness, however, and its search for food that wasn't too fast or well-defended gave Alex a few bad moments. He never knew when the eagle might go after domestic prey on the farm of someone not so sympathetic as his father.

Things are a lot different around Hawk Mountain from what they were forty years ago. For one thing, the sanctuary's relationship with its farming neighbors has not been hurt by the fact that Alex is a farmer's son and knows farming himself, and a few years back he chanced on a project that brought him in direct contact with many farmers and improved the local understanding of birds of prey. Alex wanted to see how great an effect he could have on the area's breeding population of kestrels, so he started visiting various farms to arrange to put up nesting boxes for the little falcons. That meant, as it turned out, selling the sanctuary's message each time, and doing a lot of listening in return. Two hundred boxes were put up, and the project was a success all around; before long, farmers were stopping Alex to tell him what was doing with their personal kestrels. But kestrels eat mice and small birds and insects; a golden eagle going after small farm animals might be quite a different matter.

Barbara Lake lives next door to a farmer who raises Leghorn chickens. "He's an old-fashioned farmer," says Alex. "He raises them in a brood house and he puts them outside on the range. A lot of them get up in the peach trees and the apple trees, and then they stay there at night. Some go into their rain shelters, and he closes them in, but the ones that are up in the trees, why, he just leaves them there. So, by God, that eagle learned to catch chickens, early in the morning or late in the evening. The man lost two or three chickens, you know, and he told Barbara about the eagle up there, catching his chickens. As soon as I learned about it, I quick went down to see him, and I says, 'If that eagle catches any chickens, we'll pay you whatever the chickens cost.' 'Well,' he says, 'you don't have to worry about that eagle any more.' I thought, 'Oh, my God, did he shoot it?' He says, 'I put all the chickens inside the barn; he won't get any more.' "

One of Hawk Mountain's members, an eye specialist, was particularly interested in this eagle. The doctor had combined his profession and his hobby in a fascinating bit of research: trapping birds, banding them, and examining their eyes before he freed them again. One thing he discovered, says Alex, was that of the "odd-ball birds" that were someplace they shouldn't have been at the given time of year, most had cataracts. The doctor believed that Alex's old eagle was probably suffering from the same complaint. After it had been around the neighborhood for two years, the Hawk Mountain staff tried several times to trap it, to give the doctor a look at it. But the eagle wasn't caught that summer; the hawking season began at the sanctuary —eliminating any free time for trapping expeditions— and that fall a man hunting crows at a nearby lake shot the eagle.

As for the few golden eagles that regularly spend winters in the area—something that began happening only fifteen or so years ago—one attraction must be the eagle feeding station on the Nagy farm. Alex's father hauls his dead calves up on a hillside for the birds of prey to feast on. Recently, one of his neighbors has begun to do the same thing. The eagles find the carrion, and local birders collect at a respectful distance to watch, certainly getting a longer look at this rare bird than most people ever have in a lifetime.

The numbers of golden eagles seen migrating past the mountain each fall have declined by about three-quarters in the last twenty years. This may be due to chance, the vagaries of the count; there may be some population cycle in operation that no one knows about. But it is quite likely the lower counts represent a real decline. It is questionable what effect the persistent pesticides have had on the golden eagles in eastern North America. Dieldrin apparently did considerable damage in Scotland when it was used in sheep-dips, but eastern North America is not sheep country. Whatever the effect of organochlorines on this population, human disturbance must be as important and is probably more important a factor. As a general rule, the eagles are easily upset during the nesting season by human activity, and the surviving population in the Northeast must therefore be well off the beaten track in summer. A few nests are said to be still active in the Adirondacks, their locations known only to a very few people sworn to secrecy. There are probably not many of those—known and unknown—in the eastern United States, and most of Hawk Mountain's 20 or 30 migrants a year probably come from Canada, from as far north as Ungava, east of Hudson's Bay.

The rain is over; so, it would seem, is the day's flight. Gradually, our few companions depart. Frank and I are determined to be the last watchers off the mountain this evening—to share the solitude as between friends, but otherwise to assume, each of us alone, possession of the space around us. This is the best part of the day: the silence, the aloneness, the clarity and glow of light distilling and magnifying the essence of the season, the essence of the place.

To the north, over Second Mountain on the far side of the broad valley, or to the east, up the Kittatinny ridge, or beyond the Pinnacle and the Donat, there may be a few hawks still in the air, or an eagle or two, headed toward us. The sky is for the moment empty of birds, and has been for more than an hour. But it is full of gray clouds, full of wind. The trees on the ridge before us bend in the wind, and blown leaves fly southward across our view. Except for a few autos crawling the roads far below, the valley has settled into its evening tableau.

I don't know what Frank is thinking, but I am musing about change. Here is Hawk Mountain, a small zigzag in the Kittatinny, where a sanctuary was created to protect migrating hawks from the shotguns of a few hundred hunters. It was just one gunning spot removed from the dozens along the ridge in those days, and one out of hundreds in the country, and yet the very act of its becoming a sanctuary went a long way toward stopping the hawk shooting everywhere. So the hawks are safer from shot than they used to be. Yet to protect them from what else threatens them today seems much more difficult. Pollution of the land and the air and the water would have to stop: millions of acres of sanctuary—not 1,400, as in 1934—would have to be set aside and protected not from gunners but from the urbanizers and recreationists.

One can see, even from this quiet lookout over farm countryside, what is happening. Out to the north, one of our landmarks, the Junkyard, with its burden of dead cars, epitome of our no-deposit no-return technology. House trailers and Model Homes, popping up—"overnight, like

mushrooms," as Alex puts it—on the edges of farms and
on the flanks of the mountains. What was wilderness becomes rural becomes suburban becomes urban. What's to
stop us from cementing the planet from pole to pole? Not
any moral sense, or reason, probably. Most likely famine,
plague, and war; and meanwhile, we've got ours, right?
These long-haired kids, let *them* worry about it.

From the west, another line of showers moves toward
the mountain, and Frank and I put on our ponchos. When
the rain begins, he settles into his niche between boulders,
content to wait it out. But I am convinced that, coming
this late in the day, after an hour and a half with no hawks,
the rain will put a stopper on what might have remained of
the day's flight. I rise from my rock and stuff my gear into
the pack, and after a brief debate, Frank agrees I am probably right. We are no sooner off the top of the mountain,
naturally, than the shower is over, and we nearly turn
back. But the day is about gone, and we continue down
the stony path through the aspens and oaks and rhododendron, and come out into the view again at South Lookout.

The sky is clearing, and the wind is sweeping the clouds
away overhead. We scan along the purple-black ridge
leading to North Lookout, just in case a late eagle has appeared; there are no birds in sight. We turn to continue
down toward the road, and pause for a moment beside the
roofed bulletin board that stands behind the lookout. As
we talk, a big, gray hawk streaks out of the woods—
low, only a few feet from us—and heads up along the
trail to the first bend, where it vanishes into the trees. We
shout "Goshawk!" at each other, and hurry back to the
edge of the lookout for another scan of the distant ridge.

There is a marsh hawk coming our way off that ridge,

and I follow it with my binoculars as it passes over us, quite high. Frank, meanwhile, has found a golden eagle stroking along the tops of the trees toward the upper watch. We have a pretty good argument over identification until we discover we are looking at different birds, and before I can pick up the eagle in my glasses, it slides out of sight on the far side of the ridge—to pass, as Frank wryly points out, close by the perch we left 20 minutes ago. Beyond the empty North Lookout, the last of the day's sunlight has turned a distant cloud reef to bronze. The end of the day is a crescendo of fleeing grays, golds, purples, blues, the carmine of sunset, the whistling wind, the stolid silhouette of mountain, and space.

Bibliography

Bibliography

Much material was drawn from the *News Letters* and annual reports of the Hawk Mountain Sanctuary Association. In addition:

ALLEN, R. P., and R. T. PETERSON, "The hawk migration at Cape May Point, New Yersey." *Auk*, 53(4), 1936.

ANDERSON, D. W., and J. J. HICKEY, "Eggshell changes in certain North American birds." *Proceedings XVth International Ornithological Congress*, Karl H. Voous, ed. Leiden, E. J. Brill. In press.

ARMSTRONG, EDWARD A., *The Folklore of Birds*. 2d ed. New York, Dover: 1970.

AUDUBON, JOHN JAMES, *The Birds of America*, vol. 1. New York, Dover: 1970.

AUSTING, G. RONALD, *The World of the Red-tailed Hawk*. Philadelphia and New York, Lippincott: 1964.

BAGG, AARON M., "Flight over the valley: Connecticut Valley hawk flights—September, 1948." *The Bulletin of the Massachusetts Audubon Society*, 33(4), 1949.

———, "Minimum temperatures and maximum flights: Connecticut Valley hawk flights—September, 1949." *Bull. Mass. Aud. Soc.*, 34(2), 1950.

———, "Watch New England hawk flights!" *Bull. Mass. Aud. Soc.*, 31(2), 1947.

BENT, ARTHUR CLEVELAND, *Life Histories of North American Birds of Prey*. Washington, Government Printing Office: 1937, 1938; New York, Dover: 1961.

BLANCHAN, NELTJE, *Birds That Hunt and Are Hunted*. New York, Doubleday, Page: 1902.

BREWSTER, WILLIAM, *Concord River: Selections from the Journals of William Brewster*, Smith O. Dexter, ed. Cambridge, Harvard U. Press: 1937.

————, *October Farm: From the Concord Journals and Diaries of William Brewster*. Cambridge, Harvard U. Press: 1936.

BROUN, MAURICE, *Hawks Aloft: The Story of Hawk Mountain*. New York, Dodd, Mead: 1949.

————, "Pennsylvania's bloody ridges." *Nature*, June–July, 1956.

BROWN, LESLIE, *Eagles*. New York, Arco; London, Arthur Barker, Ltd.: 1970.

————, and Dean Amadon, *Eagles, Hawks and Owls of the World*. New York, McGraw-Hill: 1968.

BRUNS, ELDON H., "Winter predation of golden eagles and coyotes on pronghorn antelopes." *Canadian Field-Naturalist*, 84(3), 1970.

CADE, T. J., *et al.*, "DDT residues and eggshell changes in Alaskan falcons and hawks." *Science*, 172(3986), 1971.

CADE, T. J., and RICHARD FYFE, "The North American peregrine survey, 1970." *Canadian Field-Naturalist*, 84(3), 1970.

CHAPMAN, FRANK M., *Camps and Cruises of an Ornithologist*. New York, D. Appleton: 1908.

————, *Handbook of Birds of Eastern North America*. New York, D. Appleton: 1939; Dover: 1966.

COLLINS, HENRY H., "Hawk slaughter at Drehersville." *Bulletin of the Hawk and Owl Society*, 1(3), 1933.

COON, N. C., *et al.*, "Causes of bald eagle mortality, 1960–1965." *Journal of Wildlife Diseases*, 6, 1970.

CRAIGHEAD, JOHN J., and FRANK C. CRAIGHEAD, JR., *Hawks, Owls and Wildlife*. New York, Dover: 1969.

EATON, ELON HOWARD, *Birds of New York*, part 2. Albany, University of the State of New York: 1914.

EPSTEIN, H. J., "The origin and earliest history of falconry." *Isis*, 34, 1944.

FISHER, A. K., *The Hawks and Owls of the United States in Their*

Relation to Agriculture. U.S. Department of Agriculture, Division of Ornithology and Mammalogy. Bulletin No. 3. Washington, Government Printing Office: 1893.

FORBUSH, EDWARD HOWE, *Birds of Massachusetts and Other New England States*, vol. 2. Norwood, Mass., Norwood Press, for the Commonwealth of Massachusetts: 1927.

GLASIER, PHILLIP, *As the Falcon Her Bells*. New York, E. P. Dutton: 1964.

GORDON, SETON, *The Golden Eagle: King of Birds*. London, Collins: 1955.

GROSSMAN, MARY LOUISE, and JOHN HAMLET, *Birds of Prey of the World*. New York, Clarkson N. Potter: 1964.

HAGAR, JOSEPH A., "Hawks at Mount Tom." *Massachusetts Audubon Bulletin*, 21, 1937.

HAUGH, JOHN RICHARD, *A Study of Hawk Migration and Weather in Eastern North America*. Ann Arbor, University Microfilms: 1971.

HERRICK, FRANCIS H., "Nests and nesting habits of the American eagle." *Auk*, 41, 1924.

HICKEY, J. J., ed., *Peregrine Falcon Populations: Their Biology and Decline*. Madison, University of Wisconsin Press: 1969.

———, and D. W. ANDERSON, "Chlorinated hydrocarbons and eggshell changes in raptorial and fish-eating birds." *Science*, 162(3850), 1968.

KEITH, J. A., and I. M. GRUCHY, "Residue levels of chemical pollutants in North American birdlife." Canadian Wildlife Service. Pesticide Section Manuscript Report No. 22, 1971.

KENNEDY, ROBERT SENIOR, "Population dynamics of ospreys in tidewater Virginia, 1970–1971." Master's thesis, William and Mary, 1971.

KRANTZ, W. C., *et al.*, "Organochlorine and heavy metal residues in bald eagle eggs." *Pesticides Monitoring Journal*, 3(8), 1970.

LYDEKKER, RICHARD, ed., *Library of Natural History*, vol. 4. New York, Akron, and Chicago, Saalfield: 1904.

MAY, JOHN B., *The Hawks of North America*. New York, National Association of Audubon Societies: 1935.

MICHELL, E. B., *The Art and Practice of Hawking*. Boston, Charles T. Branford: 1959.

MILLER, MORTON W., and GEORGE G. BERG, eds., *Chemical Fallout: Current Research on Persistent Pesticides.* Springfield, Ill., Charles C. Thomas: 1969.

MULHERN, B. M., *et al.*, "Organochlorine residues and autopsy data from bald eagles, 1966–68." *Pesticides Monitoring Journal,* 4(3), 1970.

MUTCHLER, THOMAS, "Intramedullary pinning of long bone fractures in raptors." Hawk Mountain Sanctuary Association *News Letter to Members,* No. 44, 1972.

NOLAN, J. BENNETT, ed., *Southeastern Pennsylvania: A History of the Counties of Berks, Bucks, Chester, Delaware, Montgomery, Philadelphia, and Schuylkill,* vols. 1, 2. Philadelphia, New York, Lewis Historical Publishing Co.: 1943.

PEAKALL, DAVID B., "Pesticides and the reproduction of birds." *Scientific American,* 222(4), 1970.

PEARSON, T. GILBERT, ed., *Birds of America,* vol. 2. New York, University Society: 1917.

———, "The case of the hawk." National Association of Audubon Societies. Circular No. 17, 1929.

PORTER, RICHARD D., and STANLEY N. WIEMEYER, "Dieldrin and DDT: effects on sparrow hawk eggshells and reproduction." *Science,* 165, 1969.

POSTUPALSKY, SERGEJ, "Toxic chemicals and declining bald eagles and cormorants in Ontario." Canadian Wildlife Service. Pesticide Section Manuscript Report No. 20, 1971.

POUGH, RICHARD H., letter to *Bird-Lore,* 34, Nov.–Dec., 1932.

———, "A glider highway." *Bird-Lore,* 37, Sept.–Oct., 1935.

REICHEL, W. L., *et al.*, "Pesticide residues in eagles." *Pesticides Monitoring Journal,* 3(3), 1969.

SPRUNT, ALEXANDER, JR., *North American Birds of Prey.* New York, Bonanza: 1955.

STICKEL, LUCILLE F., "Organochlorine pesticides in the environment." Department of the Interior, Fish and Wildlife Service, Bureau of Sports Fisheries and Wildlife. Special Scientific Report—Wildlife No. 119, Oct., 1968.

———, and Leon I. Rhodes, "The thin eggshell problem." *The Biological Impact of Pesticides in the Environment: Proceedings of the Symposium.* Corvallis, Oregon State University: 1970.

STONE, WITMER, *Bird Studies at Old Cape May: An Ornithology of Coastal New Jersey*. Delaware Valley Ornithological Club: 1937.

SUTTON, GEORGE MIKSCH, "Notes on a collection of hawks from Schuylkill County, Pennsylvania." *Wilson Bulletin*, 40, 1928.

——, "The status of the Goshawk in Pennsylvania." *Wilson Bulletin*, 43, 1931.

TAYLOR, ROBERT LEWIS, "Oh, Hawk of Mercy" [profile of Rosalie Barrow Edge]. *The New Yorker*, April 17, 1948.

WARREN, B. H., *Report on the Birds of Pennsylvania*, 2d ed. Harrisburg, E. K. Meyers: 1890.

WETMORE, ALEXANDER, et al., *Water, Prey, and Game Birds of North America*. Washington, National Geographic Society: 1965.

WIEMEYER, STANLEY N., and RICHARD D. PORTER, "DDT thins eggshells of captive American kestrels." *Nature*, 227(5259), 1970.

WILSON, ALEXANDER, and CHARLES LUCIAN BONAPARTE, *American Ornithology: or The Natural History of the Birds of the United States*. Popular edition, George Ord, ed. Philadelphia, Porter & Coates: n.d.

WURSTER, CHARLES F., "Effects of Insecticides." *Congressional Record*, E8333 ff., July 28, 1971.